Stashbusters!

Featuring the Controlled Scrappy Technique

9 QUILT PROJECTS

Sarah Maxwell and Dolores Smith

Stashbusters

Featuring the Controlled Scrappy Technique

Sarah Maxwell and Dolores Smith

Publisher: Amy Marson
Creative Director: Gailen Runge
Editor: Kent Richards
Technical Editor: Deanna Hodson
Book Designer: Bob Deck
Photography: Aaron T. Leimkuehler
Illustrator: Lon Eric Craven
Photo Editor: Jo Ann Groves

Published by Kansas City Star Quilts, an imprint of C&T Publishing, Inc., P.O. Box 1456 , Lafayette, CA 94549

KANSAS CITY
STAR QUILTS
an imprint of C&T Publishing

Library of Congress Cataloging-in-Publication Data

Maxwell, Sarah, 1964
Smith, Dolores, 1965

Stashbusters!: Featuring the Controlled Scrappy Technique / Sarah Maxwell and Dolores Smith

ISBN 978-1-61745-334-2
eBook ISBN 978-1-61745-335-9

Library of Congress Control Number: 2016931691

Printed in the United States of America by Walsworth Publishing Co., Marceline, MO

TABLE OF CONTENTS

DEDICATIONS

I would like to dedicate this book to my best friend, my husband Brian. There is that saying "There is someone out there for everyone, it is a matter of finding them." Well, I actually met my soul mate three times growing up. So guessing that three times is a charm, I can't say enough about how he has encouraged me and let me always follow my dreams. And to our son Kyle, whom we have watched grow into an adult over the years. Just when you think your children are not listening to you, you turn around and have a smile on your face and tears in your eyes from amazement. And lastly, to my special guardian angels Ryan and Breigha.

— Dolores

This book is dedicated to my family: my husband, Joe and daughters Megan and Shannen. Without your support, I could not accomplish all that I do. Thanks for putting up with the piles of fabric from having too many projects going at once that threaten to overtake our house, too many meals "to go," and the general chaos and craziness of my schedule. You let me live my dream and I can't express how much your support means to me.

All my love,

Sarah

ABOUT THE AUTHORS

After years of visiting quilt shows and stores around the country, Sarah Maxwell and Dolores Smith decided to open their own store in 2002. Homestead Hearth has grown to occupy most of its 10,000 square foot building over the years. The store is known for its numerous and unique block of the month selections and its focus on reproduction fabrics.

Their quilt designs regularly appear in McCall's Quilting and McCall's Quick Quilts as well as other quilting publications. They also design patterns and have authored several books for the Kansas City Star.

Sarah lives in Mexico, Missouri with her husband, Joe, and has two daughters, Megan and Shannen.

Dolores also lives in Mexico, Missouri with her husband, Brian, and has two sons, Ryan and Kyle. Dolores recently welcomed a new addition to the family, daughter-in-law Dharti, following Kyle's marriage.

Sarah Maxwell (left) and Dolores Smith (right)

ACKNOWLEDGEMENTS

Each time we write a book we are so grateful to all of the people actually involved behind the scenes. Writing and publishing a book truly requires an army of people, many of whom work or contribute without recognition. This book could not have happened without the following people:

As longtime residents of Mexico, Missouri, we're always excited to share our small town with the world. We have some real treasures in this community, one of which is the incredible Barnes House where the quilts were photographed. Dene and Mike Myers have done an incredible job of restoring this home to its current state of beauty. Thanks Dene and Mike for opening your home to us and allowing us to share it with the world.

Quilts require fabric. We are so grateful to Marcus Fabrics™, Moda Fabrics and Andover Fabrics for graciously providing much of the cloth used in our quilts.

All authors need a good editor, someone who can tactfully make suggestions and improve upon the author's original vision. Kent Richards has been a joy to work with. His professionalism and friendly attitude made working on this book a real pleasure.

Proofing and technical editing is the key to an accurate book, and we appreciate Deanna Hodson's efforts in this regard. And to Lon Eric Craven who created the diagrams and templates for the projects - thank you!

A book is most often first pulled from a rack because something catches the reader's eye, usually a photograph. Once again, Aaron Leimkuehler has worked his magic in photographing our quilts. We thank you. Also, thanks to Jo Ann Groves for editing those photos.

Books published by Kansas City Star Quilts are renowned for their "look." We need to thank Bob Deck for so creatively designing this book and making us all look so good!

Kansas City Star Quilts, now an imprint of C&T Publishing, remains the premier publisher of quality books about quilting. Their attention to detail, gorgeous photography and layouts, and focus on substance make their books a visual and intellectual treat. We are truly honored by the opportunity to write for and be published by Kansas City Star Quilts. Thanks to Doug Weaver for his support through the years.

INTRODUCTION

One of the best perks of being a quilt shop owner is the opportunity to play with fabric on a daily basis. Experimenting with different fabric combinations is always entertaining to me, and I can spend as much time trying out options on the computer as I do actually sewing.

Because I'm so drawn to how colors and prints interact, I have always gravitated toward quilts that use many, many fabrics. While the prepackaged bundles of a complete line are always tempting, I'm always wondering "What would happen if I added three prints from this other line and five prints from that line to that bundle?"

As I've worked with fabric companies and magazines over the last 10 years, my favorite quilts are the ones that use lots of fabric—often 50 to 100 different prints—always with a plan of where different colors or values should go. This "controlled scrappy" approach lets me play with color and print and makes for interesting quilts. By combining prints from several different lines and even different styles, a quilt becomes unique, reflecting the maker's personality.

I also really like large quilts—quilts that actually fit beds. While a small project quickly leads to the satisfied feeling of finishing something, I've come to appreciate the journey of making a big quilt that I can use on a bed or fold over the back of a couch.

This book brings together all of my favorites with a series of large quilts that use lots of fabrics.

My longtime business partner, Dolores Smith, shares many of my interests but also loves working with wool. Her designs in this book showcase her flair for appliqué and combining plaids with wools or cottons.

Dolores and I hope you are inspired to gather together a large assortment of fabrics and start sewing one of these projects. The fun is in seeing how blocks emerge as you combine different prints, values and even fabric styles, following the broad color guidelines provided. When you combine many, many fabrics that one piece that seems out of place often becomes the spark that sets off the entire quilt.

— Sarah Maxwell

As quilt shop owners and frequent magazine contributors, we're often asked about our favorite notions. Here are some items we can't work without:

Aurifil Thread

After trying most threads on the market, we've both permanently switched to Aurifil 50 weight cotton Mako thread for machine piecing.

Valdani Thread

For wool appliqué, we prefer Valdani pearl cotton, generally size 12. This cotton thread is hand-dyed so the colors work wonderfully with hand-dyed wools. Size 12 is the finer/thinner size of the available weights so stitches are an accent.

Judy Martin's Point Trimmer

There are numerous ways to construct half-square triangle units and everyone seems to have a favorite. The instructions in this book outline traditional rotary cutting methods, but feel free to use whatever method you prefer.

One reason we have success with traditional rotary

cutting methods is our use of Judy Martin's Point Trimmer tool. The tool lets you trim the points from cut triangles so you have a straight edge to line up rather than a narrow point. The tool includes instructions for use. It is one of our "secrets to success" in obtaining sharp points and accurate blocks.

Clover Fork Pins

Making sure seams line up accurately is always a challenge when sewing blocks with lots of pieces. One of our favorite tricks for achieving accurate seams involves using Clover fork pins. Shaped like the tines of a fork, these pins slip into a seam on either side of a positioning pin so your points line up perfectly.

Clover Embroidery Threader

Threading needles with the thicker threads like pearl cotton can be a challenge. The Clover Embroidery Threader easily accommodates thick threads without breaking.

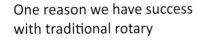

The quilts in this book are constructed with rotary cutting and machine piecing. The wool runners are constructed with machine piecing and hand appliqué. In these instructions, we will share our favorite methods and tips. Of course, feel free to adapt anything to the methods you prefer. We firmly believe that the best quilt is a finished quilt. And, we love antique and primitive quilts so we seldom worry about perfectly lining up stripes or rotating every single piece so the fabric is perfectly oriented. At the same time, we value sharp points and accurately-sized blocks. These tips should aid in achieving those goals.

Fabric

Quality of fabric makes a difference in the finished result! Your local quilt shop will generally sell top quality, 100 percent cotton fabrics suitable for piecing and quilting. If you're going to take time to make a quilt, why not invest in the best materials possible so your work lasts to pass down to those special loved ones.

Pre-washing

In all of our years of quilting, the debate of whether to pre-wash has really not changed. There will always be proponents on each side of the argument. Personally, we never pre-wash fabric. Fabric fresh off the bolt generally has a crisp feel and fewer wrinkles than something that has been washed and dried. Before cutting, we iron the fabric with a hot iron, steam and spray starch. This combination will generally reveal if any fabric is a candidate for excessive shrinking. Once a quilt is finished, dye catcher sheets such as the Shout Color Catcher can be used in the washing machine to catch any dye that isn't stable. Occasionally, if the quilt has a lot of dark colors or a lot of reds or blues which cause concern, we'll add three or four dye catcher sheets in the initial wash.

Seam Allowance

Sharp points and matching seams come down to an accurate seam allowance. Of course, you need to measure and cut accurately at the start, but if your seam allowance is off, the finished project just won't go together nicely. Take time to make sure you are

sewing with an accurate ¼" seam allowance. One simple way to make sure you have an accurate seam allowance is to cut 3 strips 1 ½" x 9". Sew them together. Measure the center strip. If it measures 1" exactly, then your seam allowance is good to go! If not, try placing a piece of tape in front of your presser foot ¼" away from where the needle hits the fabric to use as a guide and try again. Continue experimenting with placement of the tape until that center strip is 1" wide.

Pressing

In general, press seams to the darker fabric. We like to press after each piecing step. Press means flipping open a pieced unit making sure the seam allowance is going to be under the darker fabric and carefully laying a hot iron on top of the pieced unit. Avoid aggressively running the iron back and forth over the pieced unit which leads to distortion and wrinkles.

Appliqué

The templates provided in this book for appliquéd shapes show the finished edge of the piece as a dotted line. Depending on your preferred method of appliqué, you can prepare templates and appliqué as desired. For the "Tumbling We Go" project, Dolores used the freezer paper method and a whip stitch to attach the appliqué shapes to the background. Refer to your local library or quilt shop for instruction books on any appliqué method.

Freezer paper method:

1. Using the freeze paper with shiny side down trace all templates.
2. Once all templates are traced, cut out on traced line.
3. Place shiny side down on wrong side of fabric, press the shiny side onto the fabric.
4. Cut design out leaving a ¼" edge from the traced line.
5. Using a glue stick go around the edges and press the fabric edges to the freezer paper. Clipping edges around the curves.

Accuquilt® Instructions

1. Gather your Accuquilt machine, the tumbler dies & a mat of the corresponding size.

2. Lay the die on the machine.

3. Lay 1-4 layers of fabric on top of the die, making sure the shape is covered by fabric on all sides. You can use scraps and odd-sized pieces of fabric; just make sure the die edges are covered.

4. Lay a mat on top of the die and fabric.

5. Slowly crank the handle to feed the stack through the machine.

6. Remove the mat and leftover fabric to reveal your perfectly cut shapes.

TriRecs™ Instructions

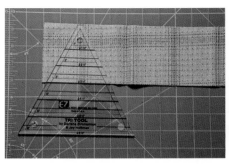

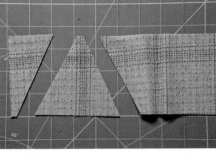

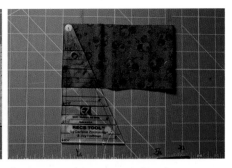

1. Cut a strip of fabric the width of the large triangle. For example, for the Pathway to the Stars quilt, cut the light and medium background fabric strips 3 ½". Lay the Tri tool on top of the strip aligning the 3 ½" marking with one edge of the strip.

2. Cut around the ruler to create "Tri" units.

3. Repeat this process for the assorted prints.

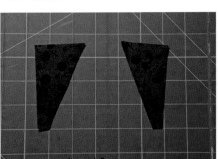

4. Reverse the ruler to create Recs units that angle in both directions.

5. Pair the Background Tri with 2 print Recs and sew together to create a finished "Tri-Recs" unit.

COLOR PHILOSOPHY and SELECTION

I'm often asked how I come up with the color or fabric combinations I use in my quilts. The best way to come up with a color plan for a quilt is to experiment, either with a quilt design program on a computer using digital fabric images or with actual fabric swatches. The obvious benefit of computer-assisted design is speed—it's much faster to switch out fabric options on a computer screen than it is to cut out and arrange block pieces. Because computers and digital processes can distort fabric colors, in the end, the choices always need to be auditioned using the actual fabrics.

There are many ways to decide on a color plan for a quilt. I'll explain a few of my favorite approaches here.

- Sarah Maxwell

FOCAL FABRIC QUILTS

Often, customers come into our store and announce they are new quilters and want to make a project but don't know where to start. After settling on a good beginner pattern, the biggest challenge for many quilters is deciding on the fabric combination. If matching a specific décor or color scheme isn't a concern, I always recommend that the customer walk around and find a fabric that she loves that has at least three or four colors in it. By identifying a "focal" fabric, we can use this print to set the tone and colors for the rest of the project.

"It's All about Love," on page 18, is a great example of a quilt designed using a focal fabric. I immediately loved the large-scale paisleys in the "Collection for a Cause-Love" line by Moda Fabrics. In particular, the blue background print beckoned to me.

Like many Moda lines, the collection included 40 prints so I was well on my way to having a big range of fabrics to use in the quilt. Another Moda collection, Historical Blenders, offered another 20 coordinates that were an exact match to the Love line. After laying all these fat quarters on my ironing board, I felt like something was missing.

Then, I noticed that the paisley print had green, lots of green, and none of the coordinates included green at all. And, red was a great accent on the paisley print, but the reds in the coordinates were all fairly similar.

By adding nine greens to the mix, the design suddenly had more interest. I selected greens in a range of value from drab olive to dark forest.

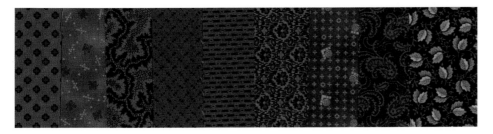

A few of the greens included red accents tying them into the focal print.

Finally, notice how the fifth green in the picture is brighter than all the other prints? While it does not technically "match" the green in the focal print, it adds a spark in the overall quilt.

Because the reds in the coordinated line were all fairly similar in value and tone, I decided to add four red prints to the mix.

The first three are darker and less orange than the coordinates. The fourth choice, which resembles floral fireworks, is again brighter than the other reds and the gold accent ties it into the focal print and the other golds used in the quilt.

I also added four blues, each with a white accent. While the coordinates all had off-white or beige accents, the pop of white again adds interest. Some people shy away from combining white and off-white or beige within a quilt. As long as you use several prints of each tone, the overall effect is pleasing.

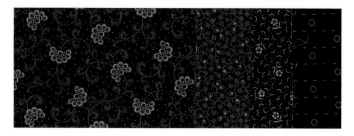

In looking at the focal print, I also knew I wanted to highlight the gold in my quilt design. Again, the coordinates had nice golds, some golden tan and some more buttery yellow.

Following my "more is always better" philosophy, I added additional golds ranging from light to dark. Some have a brown tint, others are more golden. Notice how the last two swatches incorporate accents of red and blue from the focal print. Any time a piece you add to the mix contains at least two elements from your focal print, you are almost guaranteed it will work even if it's not a perfect color match.

Finally, I focused on the backgrounds. The two Moda collections had an ample group of options, all of which had the same light beige background shade. I always prefer a range of backgrounds that actually "read" differently from a distance. So, I added several additional backgrounds ranging from very light beige to a warm, light tan. Two of the choices incorporated the darker red which I had also added to the mix.

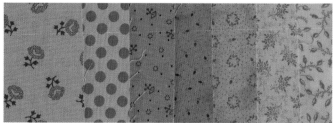

LIMITED PALETTE QUILTS

Picking a favorite color combination is another tried and true method of quilt design. There are many classics—red and white; blue and yellow; red and green; the list could go on and on. Because reproduction fabrics have long been one of my favorite genres, I gravitate toward combinations found in antique quilts. Blue and brown combined with an array of reproduction shirting fabrics is a combination I return to time and again, and it is the basis for "Blueberry and Butter."

One key to making limited palette quilts work is finding prints that incorporate both colors. Of course that can sometimes make it hard to decide which color family a print belongs in. One easy rule to follow is identify what color the background or base cloth is and assign the print to that color even if it could go either way.

An added bonus of these prints that can go either way is how much interest they add to a quilt. When you have assigned colors to a position within a block and something unexpected appears in a couple of the blocks, someone viewing the quilt will look at it longer to see what other surprises might appear.

Using stripes can have the same effect. Because stripes are generally larger-scale, when they are cut up for a quilt block, different elements or colors can appear from the same fabric.

Anytime I work with just two colors in a quilt, I make sure to pick a wide range of values within the two colors. Browns range from dark tobacco brown all the way to golden brown.

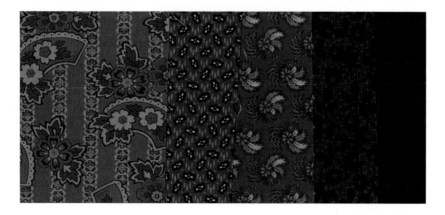

Blues range from navy to medium cadet blue.

While the blues and browns set the overall tone for "Blueberry and Butter," the wide assortment of background fabrics adds additional interest to this quilt. Shirting fabrics are reminiscent of the cloth used to make men's shirts in the 1800s. While these prints were available from numerous fabric companies in years past, more recently, they are harder to find. Therefore, I often combine them with small-scale background prints from folk art or country-style fabric lines to add a wider range of background values and more variation in the scale of the prints.

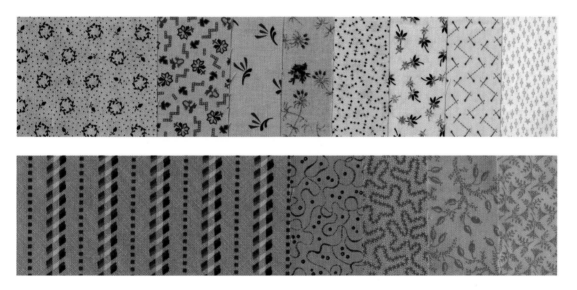

Another option I often use in designing quilts is planning where a certain color will appear in each spot in a block. I still use many different fabrics, but I always know that piece "A" will be purple or piece "B" will be a background. With this approach, more fabric choices are always better. The more fabrics appearing in the quilt overall, the more those quirky or not-quite-matching pieces will blend in overall. Additionally, it makes the sewing easy. If a blue triangle is always joined to a black triangle, I literally pick up one of each and sew them together, not worrying about whether the two fabrics match perfectly or are the same style. Once they are sewn into a block and then into the quilt, any combinations that are a little "off" will actually add interest.

"Scrappy is as Scrappy Does" is a great example of a controlled placement scrap quilt. The quilt began with my desire to use a collection of dressing gown prints designed by Judie Rothermel for Marcus Fabrics™. These fabrics are reminiscent of women's robes or dressing gowns from the 1800s and generally showcase small, delicate motifs in soft shades on a variety of creams and pastels.

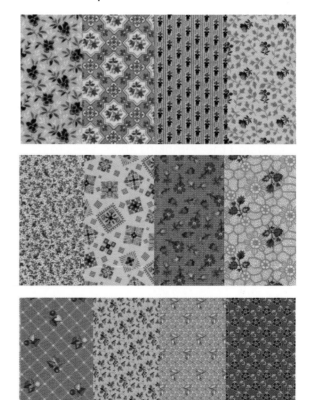

Because the dressing gowns fabrics incorporated so many colors, I decided the blocks should include a big assortment of color as well. Planning where each color would appear would help control the randomness of color placement and lend some order to the overall design.

As explained in the pattern, black and red anchored the Odd Fellow's Chain blocks in the quilt. Because most of the dressing gown fabrics included some shade of blue, the color was a natural choice to anchor the Odds & Ends block. Since black and red were featured in one of the blocks and they are strong colors, I decided on a black and red stripe for the border to tie the whole quilt together.

As explained earlier, selecting a wide range of tones and shades is essential to making this scrappy approach work. Reds range from bright reds with pink undertones to dark brick reds.

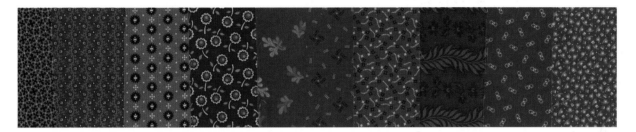

Because the block centers looked a little dull when they were all shades of gold, I added in some pumpkin and some green—both colors with yellow undertones.

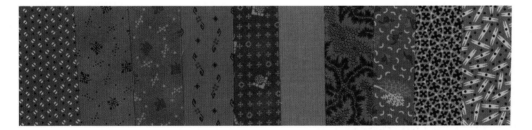

Finally, the centers of the Odds & Ends blocks were originally shades of pink, again to draw out a predominant color of the dressing gown prints. After deciding to add the pumpkins and greens to the gold color position, it was an easy decision to add purple and a touch of brown to the pink position.

Each of the quilt patterns includes some additional discussion of why colors or fabrics were selected. The most important rule of all: have fun! If you like it, that's all that matters.

IT'S ALL ABOUT LOVE

Designed and pieced by Sarah Maxwell

Custom machine quilting by Connie Gresham

Finished size: 103" x 114"

When the Collection for a Cause-Love line from Moda debuted, the gorgeous paisley floral immediately called out to be the focal point of a quilt. The blues and reds combined with green and gold suggested that a quilter could span the rainbow in selecting colors for a project using this fabric.

This type of large-scale, multicolor print easily sets the color tone for a project. Just look for coordinating prints in a variety of sizes and similar colors. Obvious choices are the companion prints from the same line, but it's more fun to seek out prints from other lines to add more interest and get away from the "matchy-matchy" feeling that comes from a quilt made solely from a single line of fabrics.

"It's All About Love" features 90—8" finished double four-patch blocks. The pieced blocks alternate with plain setting squares of the focal fabric letting the focal print set the overall tone and feel of the quilt.

FABRIC REQUIREMENTS

- 2 yards total of assorted light prints for double four-patch backgrounds
- 2 yards total of assorted medium and dark prints for double four-patch accents
- 3 ½ yards total of assorted gold and tan prints for double four-patch blocks
- 6 ¾ yards of blue floral for setting squares, setting triangles, setting corners and binding

Note: Because my personal fabric and quilt philosophy is always "more is better," I used more than 50 different fabrics in the quilt. If you want to replicate the quilt as shown, use scraps or buy the smallest cut possible (a fat quarter or a fat eighth) and cut pieces for just one or two blocks from each fabric and save the remaining fabric for future projects.

CUTTING INSTRUCTIONS

Block cutting instructions below are for one block only. For each double four-patch block, select two light background prints, two medium or dark prints and one gold or tan print.

From each **light print**, cut:
- 2—2 ½" squares for a total of four (two pairs of two) squares for block

From each **medium or dark print**, cut:
- 2—2 ½" squares for a total of four (two pairs of two) squares for block

From **gold or tan print**, cut:
- 2—4 ½" squares

From **blue floral focal print**, cut:
- 72—8 ½" squares, for setting squares
- 9—12 ½" squares, then cut each in half diagonally twice for a total of 36 setting triangles (there will be two extra triangles)
- 2—6 ½" squares, then cut each in half diagonally once for a total of four corner triangles
- 11—2 ½" strips the width of fabric for binding

SEWING INSTRUCTIONS

Blocks

1 | With right sides together, layer a light print square with a medium or dark print square. Using a ¼" seam allowance, sew along one side of the squares to create a pieced rectangular unit. Press toward the dark print. Repeat to make two pairs of matching pieced units for a total of four pieced units.

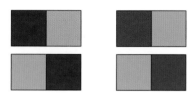

2 | Referring to the following diagram, sew together two matching pieced units from step 1 to form a four-patch.

3 | Repeat with the other set of pieced units to make a second four-patch.

4 | Sew a gold or tan square to each four-patch. Press seam toward the gold or tan print.

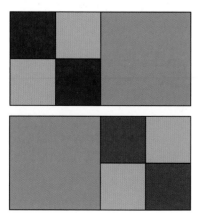

5 | Referring to the diagram below, sew the pieced units together to form a double four-patch.

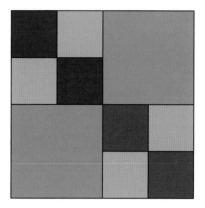

6 | Repeat steps 1—5 to make a total of 90 double four-patch blocks, varying the fabric combinations with each block. The block should measure 8" finished and 8 ½" unfinished.

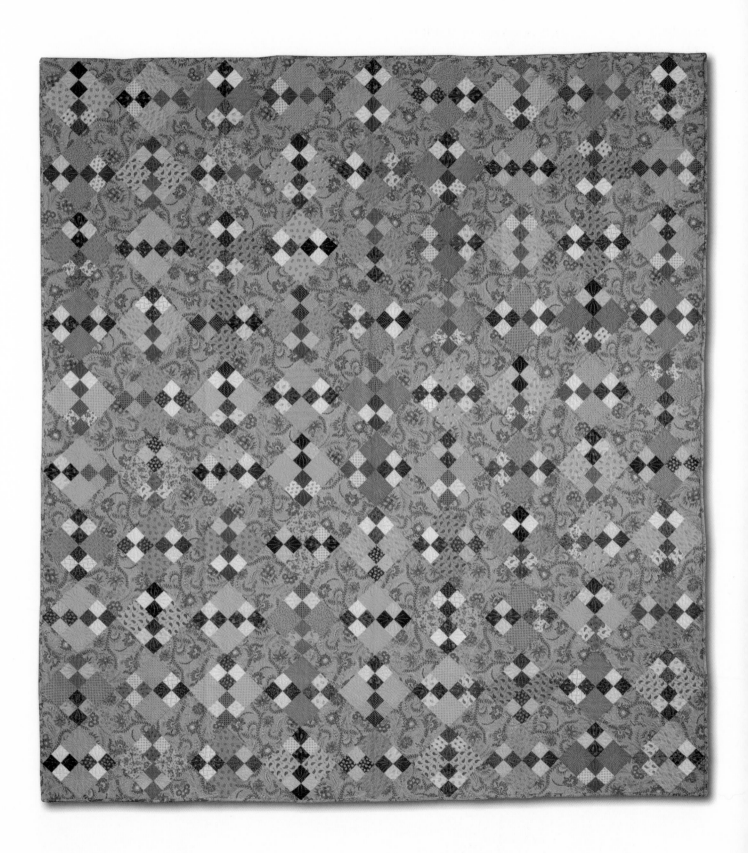

QUILT ASSEMBLY

1 | Referring to the quilt assembly diagram on page 23, lay out the double four-patch blocks, setting squares, setting triangles, and corner triangles.

2 | Referring to the quilt assembly diagram, sew the blocks together in diagonal rows, paying careful attention to the orientation of the blocks. The small four-patch unit in the blocks alternates between horizontal and vertical placement in each block. Press the seams of each row in alternate directions.

3 | Join the rows to complete the quilt center, which should measure 102" x 113".

4 | Because this quilt has no border, we recommend that you stay stitch the edges to prevent distortion and fraying during the quilting process. Simply stitch around the entire outer edge of the quilt a scant ¼" from the edge so the stitches will be covered by your binding.

5 | Sandwich the quilt top, batting, and backing; baste. Quilt as desired, then bind.

It's All About Love

quilt assembly diagram

SUMMER GONE BY

Designed and pieced by Sarah Maxwell

Custom machine quilting by Connie Gresham

Finished size: 110" x 127"

1800s reproduction fabrics have long been my biggest obsession. After years of collecting, I finally decided to start using them. Instead of keeping collections neatly bundled together, I planned this quilt, reached into the closet and just picked colors and prints I loved. Often people associate reproduction fabrics with dark, drab tones. In reality, 1800s prints span the rainbow with bright pops of double pink, poison green, chrome yellow and cheddar. The Double Pinwheel block let me pair fabrics in groups of three, playing with colors and prints. While I'm drawn to pre-packaged bundles of complete collections like most quilters, I most enjoy pulling out a few prints from several collections and seeing how they play together.

"Summer Gone By" features 72—10" finished Double Pinwheel blocks set on point and separated by sashing. Many of the quilts in this book are large. With a king-sized bed, a pillow top mattress and a tall box spring, finding quilts to fit my bed has always been a challenge. Part of the focus of this book is quilts that actually fit today's beds. While you can always make more blocks to increase the size of a quilt, one trick to increasing size without making more blocks is to set them on point. The diagonal measurement of a quilt block is always larger than its sides (by a factor of 1.414 if you are math-inclined). So this 10" block suddenly takes up the same area as approximately a 14" block when set on point. Add some sashing to separate the blocks and you easily have a quilt to fit a bed.

FABRIC REQUIREMENTS

- 5 ⅝ yards total of assorted medium and dark prints in a range of colors and prints for blocks*
- 2 ¾ yards of assorted backgrounds for blocks
- ⅝ yard of red print for cornerstones
- 3 ½ yards of stripe for sashing
- 3 ½ yards of small-scale floral for setting triangles and outer border
- 1 yard of pink print for binding

*Note: I used about 80 different prints in this quilt. From most of the medium and dark fabrics I cut only one set of Piece A triangles and one set of Piece B triangles—a 7" x 20" piece of fabric would be ideal. If you're working with fat quarters, consider cutting the Piece A and Piece B triangles which will leave you with approximately 10" x 20" from the fat quarter. Of course, you can put this extra away in your stash. Once I've taken the time to iron my fabric and have it out, I like to go ahead and cut the extra yardage into pieces I will use in the future. I have several scrap quilts "in progress" so I can always use certain shapes and sizes in the future. For me, any time I have leftover 1800s reproduction prints, I first cut a 2 ½" wide strip to be used in a future chain-style quilt. Then I cut a strip of 2 ½" finished half-square triangles. I have a design underway that needs, literally, thousands of HSTs, so I can always use those. Finally, if any yardage is left, I cut a 1 ½" strip to be used in a log cabin design. These basic sizes/units are things I go back to time and again and it certainly makes working on a scrappy quilt easier if I already have some of the pieces cut and ready to go.

CUTTING INSTRUCTIONS

From the **assorted medium and dark prints**, cut:
- 72—6 ¼" squares then cut each in half diagonally twice, for a total of 288 triangles (A)
- 72 sets of 2 matching 5 ⅞" squares then cut each in half diagonally once, for a total of 288 triangles (B)

From the **assorted backgrounds**, cut:
- 72—6 ¼" squares then cut each in half diagonally twice, for a total of 288 triangles (A)

From the **red print**, cut:
- 5—2 ½" x width of fabric strips, subcut into 71—2 ½" squares for cornerposts.
- 1—4" x width of fabric strip, subcut into 7—4" squares, then cut each in half diagonally twice to yield 28 triangles. You will use 26 of these triangles for cornerpost triangles.

From the **stripe**, cut:
- 11—10 ½" x width of fabric strips, subcut into 168—2 ½" x 10 ½" strips

From the **small-scale floral**, cut:
- 6—15 ⅜" squares, then cut each in half diagonally twice for a total of 24 setting triangles. You will use 22 of these triangles
- 2—7 ⅞" squares, then cut each in half diagonally once for a total of four corner triangles
- 12—4 ½" x WOF strips for outer border

From the **pink print**, cut:
- 12—2 ½" x WOF strips for binding

SEWING INSTRUCTIONS

Block piecing instructions below are for one block only. Repeat to make a total of 72 blocks.

For each block, select one light background print, one medium or dark print for Triangle A and a contrasting or complementary medium or dark print for Triangle B.

Double Pinwheel Block

1 | Referring to the diagram below for placement, sew a Print (A) triangle to a Background (A) triangle. Press seams toward the medium/dark print. Make 4.

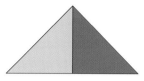

2 | Sew a Print (B) triangle to the above triangle unit. Press seams toward the B triangle. Make 4.

3 | Sew the four pieced units together to form a block. Press seams in the two rows in opposite directions.

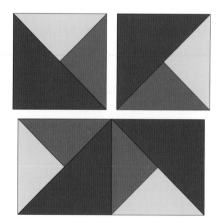

4 | Make 72 Pinwheels.

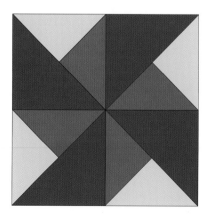

26

SUMMER GONE BY

QUILT ASSEMBLY

1 | The quilt is sewn together in diagonal rows with each block separated by a sashing strip and each row of blocks separated by a row of sashing strips and corner stones. Referring to the quilt assembly diagram below, lay out your blocks on a design wall or on the floor to ensure you are happy with your color placement. Beginning in the top left corner, sew two cornerpost triangles to opposite ends of a sashing strip. Press seams toward the cornerpost triangles.

2 | Sew a corner triangle to the top of this sashing unit.

3 | Sew a setting triangle and a sashing strip to opposite sides of a Double Pinwheel block. Press seams toward the blocks.

4 | Continue this process joining additional sashing and block rows as shown.

5 | When all of the rows are joined, the interior of the quilt should measure 102" x 119".

6 | Measure the quilt top from top to bottom through the center. Piece three strips of the outer border print end to end, then cut to match that measurement. Repeat to make a second border strip. Referring to the quilt assembly diagram, sew these strips to the sides of the quilt top. Press the seams toward the outer border.

7 | Measure the quilt top from side to side through the center (including the borders you just added). Piece three strips of the outer border print end to end, then cut to match that measurement. Repeat to make a second outer border strip. Referring to the quilt assembly diagram, sew these two strips to the top and bottom of the quilt top. Press the seams toward the outer border.

8 | Quilt as desired, then bind.

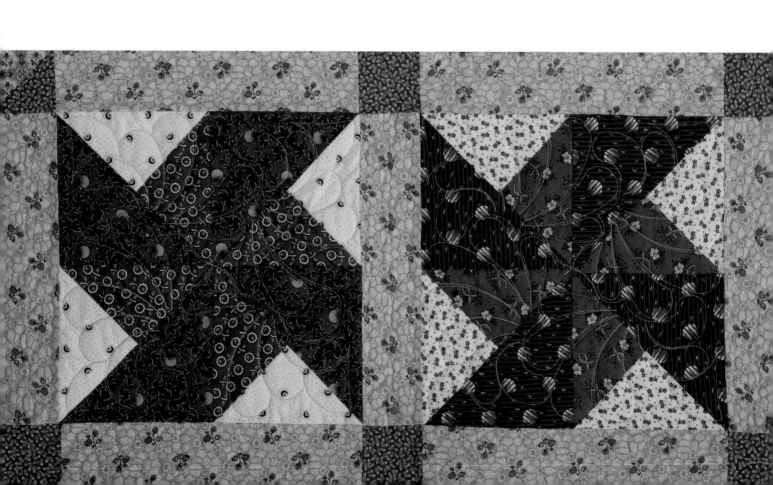

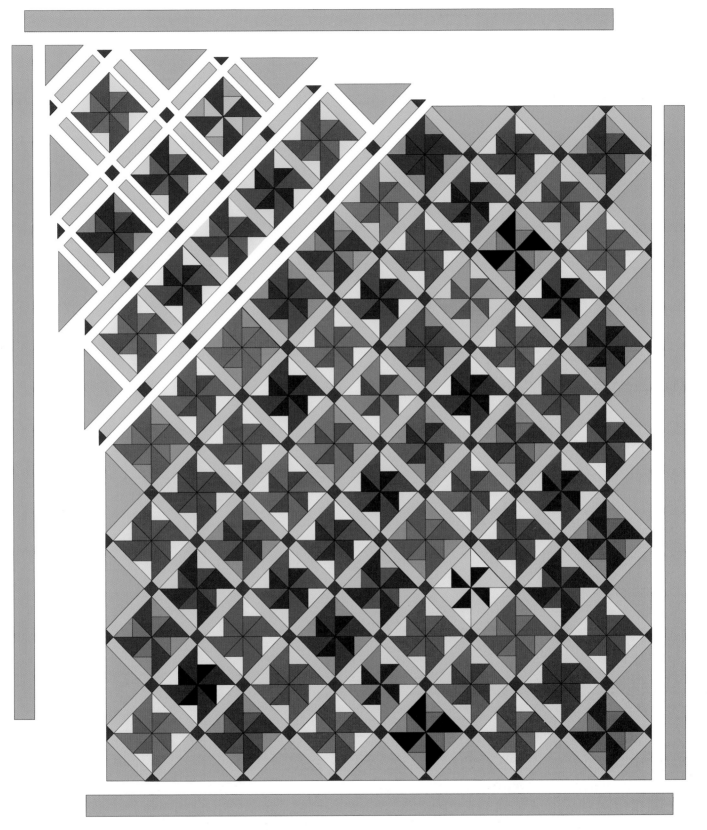

Summer Gone By

quilt assembly diagram

SCRAPPY IS AS SCRAPPY DOES

Designed by Sarah Maxwell

Pieced by Dolores Smith

Custom machine quilting by Connie Gresham

Finished size: 100" x 117"

One of my favorite types of reproduction fabrics are "dressing gown" prints — small-scale multicolor prints often on light backgrounds. These prints were often used in ladies' dressing gowns in the mid-1800s. Using these colorful, but still subdued backgrounds in place of solids or tonal backgrounds adds a lot of interest to a quilt, bringing a simple pattern to life.

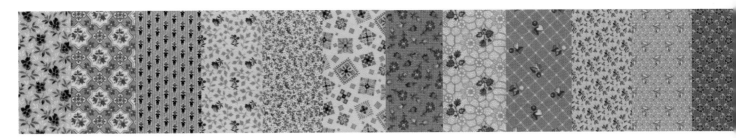

In our years of working on quilts together, Dolores and I have fallen into the routine of me often cutting out all the pieces for a quilt and Dolores assembling the blocks and top. With this project, Dolores spent some time thinking about what to name the quilt as she pieced all the half-square triangles. And, suddenly, the idea of "Scrappy is as Scrappy Does" popped into her head. While the quilt is very scrappy using more than 50 fabrics, the controlled placement of certain colors makes it easy to just pick up prints from the stash and get busy sewing. What a great way to make a dent in that stash so you have room for more!

"Scrappy Is as Scrappy Does" features 30—12" finished Odd Fellows Chain (OFC) blocks and 20—12" finished Odds & Ends (OE) blocks. The pieced are set together on point in alternating rows.

FABRIC REQUIREMENTS

- 3 ¾ yards total of assorted light prints for OFC block backgrounds
- 2 ½ yards total of assorted black prints for OFC blocks
- 1 ¾ yards total of assorted red prints for OFC blocks
- ½ yard total of assorted gold and green prints for OFC blocks
- 2 ½ yards total of assorted blue prints for OFC and OE blocks
- 3 ¾ yards total of assorted dressing gown prints for OE blocks and setting triangles and corner triangles
- 1 yard total of assorted pink and blue prints for OE blocks
- ¾ yard small-scale black print for inner border
- 2 ¼ yards of a red and black stripe for outer border
- 1 yard black print for binding

Note: Because my personal fabric and quilt philosophy is always "more is better," I used more than 50 different fabrics in the quilt. If you want to replicate the quilt as shown, use scraps or buy the smallest cut possible (a fat quarter or a fat eighth) and cut pieces for just one or two blocks from each fabric and save the remaining fabric for future projects.

CUTTING INSTRUCTIONS

Block cutting instructions below are for cutting the entire quilt at once.

For each **Odd Fellows Chain Block**, select one light background print, one red print, one black print, one blue print and one gold or green print.

From **light prints**, cut:
- 30 sets of 8 matching 2" squares, for a total of 240 Piece A squares
- 30 sets of 8 matching 2 3/8" squares then cut each in half diagonally once for a total of 480 Piece B half-square triangles
- 30 sets of 2 matching 4 1/4" squares then cut each in half diagonally twice for a total of 240 Piece C quarter-square triangles

From **blue prints**, cut:
- 30 sets of 4 matching 2 3/8" squares then cut each in half diagonally once for a total of 240 Piece B half-square triangles

From **gold or green prints**, cut:
- 30—3 1/2" Piece E squares

From **red prints**, cut:
- 30 sets of 4 matching 3 7/8" squares then cut each in half diagonally once for a total of 240 Piece D half-square triangles

From **black prints**, cut:
- 30 sets of 4 matching 2" squares, for a total of 120 Piece A squares
- 30 sets of 8 matching 2 3/8" squares then cut each in half diagonally once for a total of 480 Piece B half-square triangles

- 30—4 1/4" squares then cut each in half diagonally twice for a total of 120 Piece C quarter-square triangles

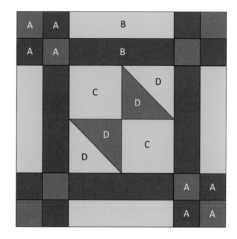

For each **Odds & Ends Block**, select one dressing gown print, one blue print and one pink or purple print.

From **dressing gown prints**, cut:
- 20 sets of 4 matching 2" x 6 1/2" rectangles for a total of 80 Piece B rectangles
- 20 sets of 2 matching 3 1/2" squares for a total of 40 Piece C squares
- 20—3 7/8" squares then cut each in half diagonally once for a total of 40 Piece D triangles

From **blue prints**, cut:
- 20 sets of 8 matching 2" squares for a total of 160 Piece A squares
- 20 sets of 4 matching 2" x 6 1/2" rectangles for a total of 80 Piece B rectangles

From **pink or purple prints**, cut:
- 20 sets of 8 matching 2" squares for a total of 160 Piece A squares
- 20—3 7/8" squares then cut each in half diagonally once for a total of 40 Piece D squares

Setting and Finishing
From **dressing gown prints**, cut:
- 5—18 1/8" squares, then cut each in half diagonally twice for a total of 20 setting triangles (there will be two extra triangles)
- 2—9 3/8" squares, then cut each in half diagonally once for a total of four corner triangles

From the **small black print**, cut:
- 12—2" strips the width of fabric for inner border

From the **red and black stripe**, cut:
- 12—6 ½" strips the width of fabric for outer border

From the **black print**, cut:
- 11—2 ½" strips the width of fabric for binding

SEWING INSTRUCTIONS

Odd Fellow's Chain Block

Block piecing instructions below are for one block only. For each OFC block, select one black print, one red print, one light background print, one gold or green print and one blue print.

Block A

1 | With right sides together, layer a light background print triangle (B) with a black print triangle (B). Using a ¼" seam allowance, sew along the long side of the triangles to make a half-square triangle unit. Press the seam toward the black print. Repeat to make a total of 8 half-square triangle units per block.

2 | Referring to the following diagram, sew together 1—light 2" square (A) to 1 half-square triangle unit. Make 4 of these units.

3 | Sew a black 2" square (A) to a half-square triangle unit. Make 4.

4 | Sew the two pieced units above together as shown. This is a "corner unit." Make 4.

5 | Sew 2 black triangles (B) to either side of 1 light triangle (C) to make a flying geese unit. Make 4 units per block.

6 | Sew a black triangle (C) to the top of the flying geese units. Make 4.

7 | Sew 2 light triangles (B) to either side of the above unit. See diagram. Make 4.

8 | Sew 2 red triangles (D) to either side of the above unit. See diagram. Make 4.

9 | Sew 2 corner units to either side of the flying geese unit. Make 2 of these top and bottom units.

10 | Sew 2 blue (B) triangles to either side of 1 light background (C) triangle. Make 4.

11 | Sew 2 light background (A) squares to either side of the 1 flying geese unit. Make 2.

12 | Sew 2 flying geese units to either side of 1 Gold or Green (E) square. Make 1.

13 | Sew these units together in rows.

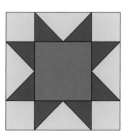

14 | Sew the flying geese units to the outside of the Star unit. See diagram.

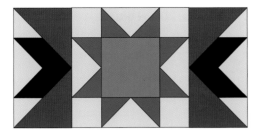

15 | Sew the top and bottom units to the star unit.

16 | Make 30 of these blocks.

Odds & Ends Block

Block piecing instructions below are for one block only. For each OE block, select one dressing gown print, one blue print, and one pink or purple print.

Four-Patch Units

1 | With right sides together, layer a pink/purple print square (A) with a blue print square (A). Using a ¼" seam allowance, sew together. Repeat with another set of squares. Make 8 sets per block.

2 | Sew the pieced squares into a four-patch unit. Make 4 per block.

Rectangles Units

3 | Sew 1 blue (B) rectangle to 1 Dressing Gown (B) rectangle together. Make 4 per block.

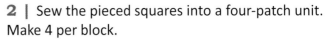

4 | Sew 1 pink or purple (D) triangle to 1 Dressing Gown (D) triangle to form a half-square triangle unit. Make 2 per block.

5 | Sew 1 half-square triangle unit to the side of a Dressing Gown square(C). See diagram below for placement. Make 2 per block.

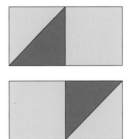

6 | Sew 2 four-patch units to either side of 1 rectangle unit. Make 2 per block.

7 | Sew 2 rectangle units to either side of center unit.

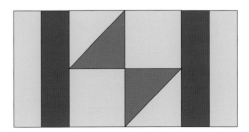

8 | Sew the rows together to form the block. Make 20.

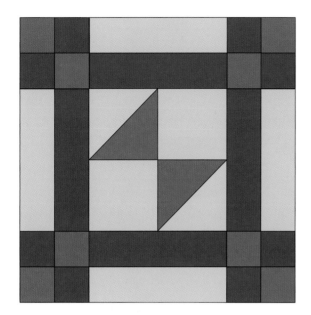

QUILT ASSEMBLY

1 | Referring to the quilt assembly diagram, lay out the 30 OFC blocks, 20 OE blocks, setting triangles and corner triangles. Sew them together into diagonal rows, being careful to match the corners. Press the seams in alternate directions.

2 | Join the rows to create the quilt center, which should measure 85" x 102".

3 | Measure the quilt center from top to bottom through the center. Piece three 2" wide inner border print strips end to end, then cut to match the measurement. Repeat to make a second inner border strip. Referring to the quilt assembly diagram, sew these two strips to the sides of the quilt center. Press the seams toward the inner border.

4 | Measure the quilt top from side to side through the center (including the borders you just added). Piece three 2" wide inner border print strips end to end, then cut to match that measurement. Repeat to make a second inner border strip. Referring to the quilt assembly diagram, sew these two strips to the top and bottom of the quilt top. Press the seams toward the inner border.

5 | Measure the quilt top from top to bottom through the center. Piece three 6 ½" wide outer border print strips end to end, then cut to match that measurement. Repeat to make a second outer border strip. Referring to the quilt assembly diagram, sew these two strips to the sides of the quilt top. Press the seams toward the outer border.

6 | Measure the quilt top from side to side through the center (including the borders you just added). Piece three 6 ½" wide outer border print strips end to end, then cut to match that measurement. Repeat to make a second outer border strip. Referring to the quilt assembly diagram, sew these two strips to the top and bottom of the quilt top. Press the seams toward the outer border.

7 | Quilt as desired, then bind.

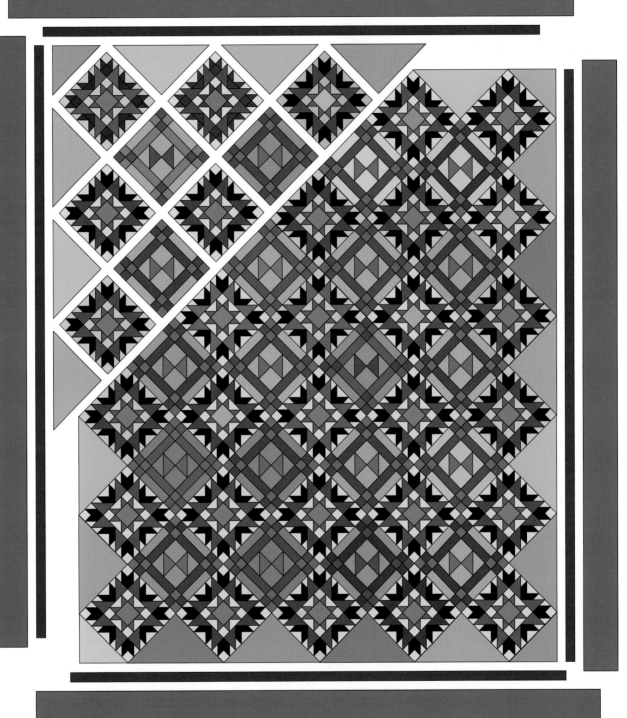

Scrappy Is As Scrappy Does
quilt assembly diagram

BLUEBERRY AND BUTTER

Designed by Sarah Maxwell

Pieced by Dolores Smith

Custom machine quilting by Connie Gresham

Finished size: 78" x 96"

A large-scale, multicolor print always catches my eye as a potential design source. When I saw the intricate paisley in the Tavern Blues 2 line by Marcus Fabrics™, I loved how the yellow highlights made the navy blue sparkle.

I decided this print could determine the color story for a quilt. While the coordinates from the line were obvious choices, I wanted to pull in other fabrics from a wide range of styles and companies. Prints designed by Jo Morton over many years blended beautifully with the Tavern collection. Combining both 1800s shirting prints and a variety of light tan florals and geometrics added interest to the nine-patch backgrounds. The mediums and darks in the nine-patches range from medium to dark navy blue and tan to dark tobacco brown.

Again working collaboratively, I designed this quilt and selected the fabrics. Dolores then pieced and assembled the top. Upon seeing the fabrics, Dolores was reminded of a time years past when she would stay with her grandpa and awake to find a breakfast of English tea and toast waiting for her. The name "Blueberry and Butter" captured the colors of the quilt.

"Blueberry and Butter" features 32—9" finished Dark Double Nine-Patch blocks alternating with 31—9" finished Light Double Nine-Patch blocks.

FABRIC REQUIREMENTS

Dark Double Nine-Patch (Block A)
- 1 ¼ yards total of assorted medium to dark blue and brown prints for nine patches
- 1 ⅛ yards total of assorted backgrounds for nine-patches
- 1 ⅞ yards of dark blue print for blocks

Light Double Nine-Patch (Block B)
- 1 ⅛ yards total of assorted medium to dark blue and brown prints for nine-patches
- 1 ¼ yards total of assorted backgrounds for nine-patches
- 1 ⅞ yards total of yellow prints for blocks
- ½ yard brown print for center of blocks
- ⅝ yard small-scale black print for inner border
- 1 ¾ yards of large-scale multi navy print for outer border
- ⅞ yard navy print for binding

CUTTING INSTRUCTIONS

Due to the very scrappy nature of this quilt, cutting instructions are for cutting one block at a time.

For each **Dark Double Nine-Patch (Block A)** select five different medium to dark blue or brown prints and five different background prints.

From **medium to dark blue and brown** prints, cut:
- 5 sets of 5 matching 1 ½" squares for a total of 25 Piece A squares

From **backgrounds**, cut:
- 5 sets of 4 matching 1 ½" squares for a total of 20 Piece A squares

From **dark blue print**, cut:
- 4—3 ½" Piece B squares

For each **Light Double Nine-Patch (Block B)** select four different medium to dark blue or brown prints and four different background prints.

From **medium to dark blue and brown prints**, cut:
- 4 sets of 4 matching 1 ½" squares for a total of 16 Piece A squares

From **backgrounds**, cut:
- 5 sets of 4 matching 1 ½" squares for a total of 20 Piece A Squares

From **yellow print**, cut:
- 4—3 ½" squares

From **brown print**, cut:
- 1—3 ½" square

From **small-scale black print**, cut:
- 8—2" strips the width of the fabric for inner border

From the **large-scale, multi print**, cut:
- 8—6 ½" strips the width of the fabric for outer border

From **navy print**, cut:
- 9—2 ½" strips the width of the fabric for binding

SEWING INSTRUCTIONS

Dark Double Nine-Patch

Block piecing instructions below are for one block only. For each dark double nine patch block, select five different medium to dark blue or brown prints and five different background prints.

1 | Referring to the diagram, sew together 5—1 ½" medium to dark blue or brown print A squares with 4—1 ½" background print A squares to create a nine-patch unit. Press seams toward the dark print.

2 | Repeat to make a total of five different nine-patch units per block.

3 | Referring to the diagram, sew together the five (5) nine-patch units from step 2, to 3 ½" dark blue print B squares to form a large nine patch. Press seams toward the large square.

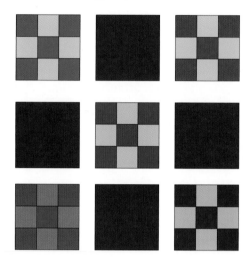

4 | The block should measure 9 ½" unfinished, 9" finished.

5 | Repeat the above steps to make 32 dark double nine-patch blocks.

BLUEBERRY AND BUTTER

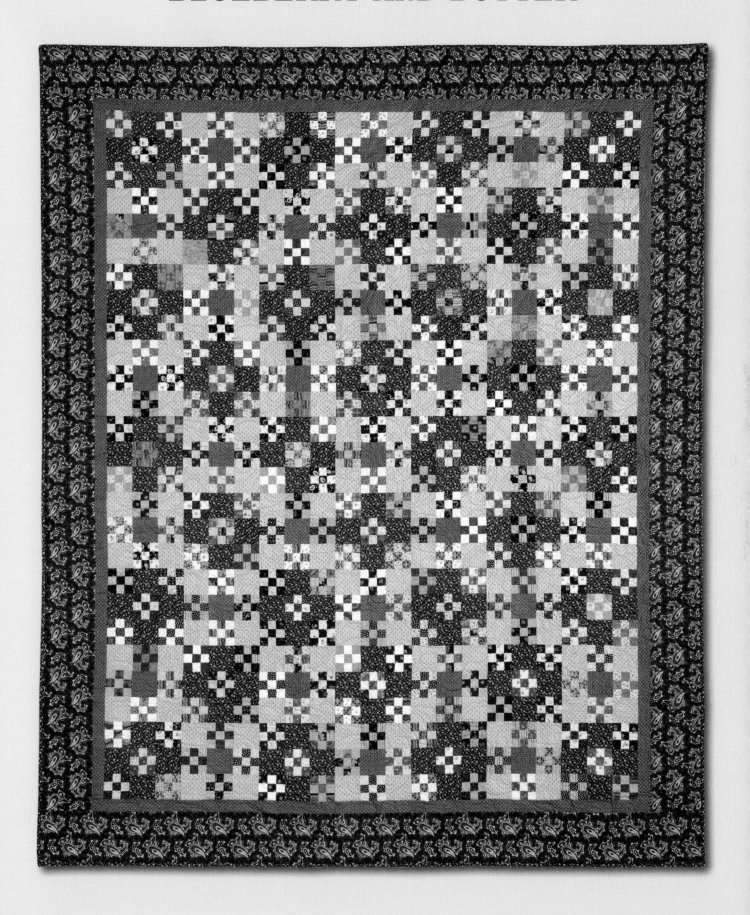

Light Double Nine-Patch

Block piecing instructions below are for one block only. For each light double nine-patch block, select four different medium to dark blue or brown prints and four different background prints.

1 | Referring to the diagram, sew together 4—1 ½" medium to dark blue or brown print A squares with 5—1 ½" background print A squares to create a nine-patch unit. Press seams toward the dark print.

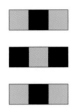

2 | Repeat to make a total of four (4) different nine-patch units per block.

3 | Referring to the following diagram, sew together four (4) nine-patch units from step 1, 4—3 ½" yellow print squares, and 1—3 ½" brown print square.

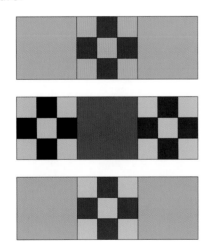

4 | The block should measure 9 ½" unfinished, 9" finished.

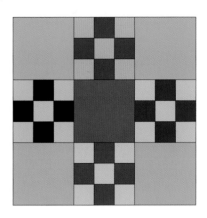

5 | Repeat the above steps to make 31 light double nine-patch blocks.

QUILT ASSEMBLY

1 | Referring to the photo of the quilt on page 41 for placement, sew a row of seven blocks, starting with a Block A and alternating with a Block B. Repeat to make a total of five (5) of these rows.

2 | Referring to the photo of the quilt on page 41 for placement, sew a row of seven blocks, starting with a Block B and alternating with a Block A. Repeat to make a total of four (4) of these rows.

3 | Referring to the quilt assembly diagram on page 43, lay out the rows from steps 1 and 2, starting with a row from step 1 and alternating with a row from step 2.

4 | Join the rows to create the quilt center. The top should measure 63 ½" x 81 ½".

5 | Measure the quilt center from the top to bottom through the center. Piece two 2" wide inner border strips end to end, then cut to match that measurement. Repeat to make a second inner border strip. Referring to the quilt assembly diagram, sew these two strips to the sides of the quilt center. Press the seams toward the inner border.

6 | Measure the quilt top from side to side through the center (including the borders you just added). Piece 2" wide inner border print strips end to end, then cut to match that measurement. Repeat to make a second inner border strip. Referring to the quilt assembly diagram, sew these strips to the top and bottom of the quilt top. Press the seams toward the inner border.

7 | Measure the quilt top from top to bottom through the center. Piece two 6 ½" wide blue print strips end to end, then cut to match that measurement. Repeat to make a second outer border strip. Referring to the quilt assembly diagram, sew these two strips to the sides of the quilt top. Press the seams toward the outer border.

8 | Measure the quilt top from side to side through the center (including the borders you just added). Piece two 6 ½" wide blue print strips end to end, then cut to match that measurement. Repeat to make a second outer border strip. Referring to the quilt assembly diagram, sew these two strips to the top and bottom of the quilt top. Press the seams toward the outer border.

9 | Quilt as desired, then bind.

Blueberry and Butter
quilt assembly diagram

TUMBLING WE GO

Designed and made
by Dolores Smith

Machine quilting by
Connie Gresham

Finished size: 82" x 96"

This quilt was made with autumn in mind. Autumn is one of my favorite times with all the leaves, pumpkins and gourds. I used flannels by Marcus Fabrics™. They have great, rich colors and they are woven plaids, one of my favorite fabric styles!

After piecing the tumblers, I appliquéd a few gourds in the lower righthand corner of the quilt top. While templates are provided for the tumbler block, I used the Accuquilt cutting system for my tumblers. Instructions on how to use it are on page 9. You will enjoy making this one.

FABRIC REQUIREMENTS

- 5 ½ yards of assorted flannel plaids
- 1 yard gold flannel for inner border and binding
- 2 ¾ yards of blue flannel for outer border
- ⅛ yard brown for gourd stems
- ⅓ yard cream for light gourds
- ¼ yard tan for middle gourd

CUTTING INSTRUCTIONS

From **assorted flannel plaids**, cut:
- 78—Large Tumblers
- 216—Small Tumblers

From **gold flannel**, cut:
- 8—1 ½" by width of fabric for inner border
- 9 – 2 ½" by width of fabric for binding

From **blue flannel**, cut:
- 4—5 ½" by **length** of fabric for outer border

SEWING INSTRUCTIONS

1 | Starting with the large tumblers, select 13 assorted prints and sew them together, alternating as shown in diagram. Make 6 rows.

2 | Sew the small tumblers together in the same manner, alternating them as shown in the diagram. Sew 24 small tumblers together to make a row. Make 9 rows.

QUILT ASSEMBLY

1 | Sew three rows of the large tumblers together as shown in the diagram. Make two sets. These rows will become the top and bottom of the quilt.

2 | Sew 9 rows of the small tumblers together as shown in the diagram. These rows are in the middle of the quilt top.

3 | Sew a set of the large tumblers to the top of the small tumblers. Sew the other set to the bottom of the small tumblers.

4 | After all the rows are sewn together, you will notice that the ends are not even. Trim both sides of the quilt to be even as shown in the quilt top diagram. The top should measure 70 ½" x 84 ½".

5 | Measure the quilt center form the top to bottom through the center. Piece two 1 ½" wide inner border strips end to end, then cut to match that measurement. Repeat to make a second inner border strip. Referring to the quilt assembly diagram on page 48, sew these two strips to the sides of the quilt center. Press the seams toward the inner border.

6 | Measure the quilt top from side to side through the center (including the borders you just added). Piece 1 ½" wide inner border strips end to end, then cut to match that measurement. Repeat to make a second inner border strip. Referring to the quilt assembly diagram on page 48, sew these strips to the top and bottom of the quilt top. Press the seams toward the inner border.

7 | Measure the quilt top from top to bottom through the center. Cut one 5 ½" wide outer border strip to this measurement (the border is cut length of fabric) and sew to the side of the quilt top. Do the same to the other side of the quilt top. Press the seams toward the outer border.

8 | Measure the quilt top from side to side through the center (including the borders you just added). Cut one 5 ½" wide outer border strip to this measurement and sew to the top of the quilt top. Repeat for the bottom border. Press the seams toward the outer border.

9 | Quilt as desired, and then bind.

APPLIQUÉ

To appliqué the gourds I used the freezer paper technique. I was shown this appliqué technique by Sarah and it's now one of my favorites. So, thank you! See general instructions for the technique.

Also, I used the whip stich instead of the traditional appliqué stitch. Templates are found on pages 49 and 76-80.

Tumbling We Go

quilt assembly diagram

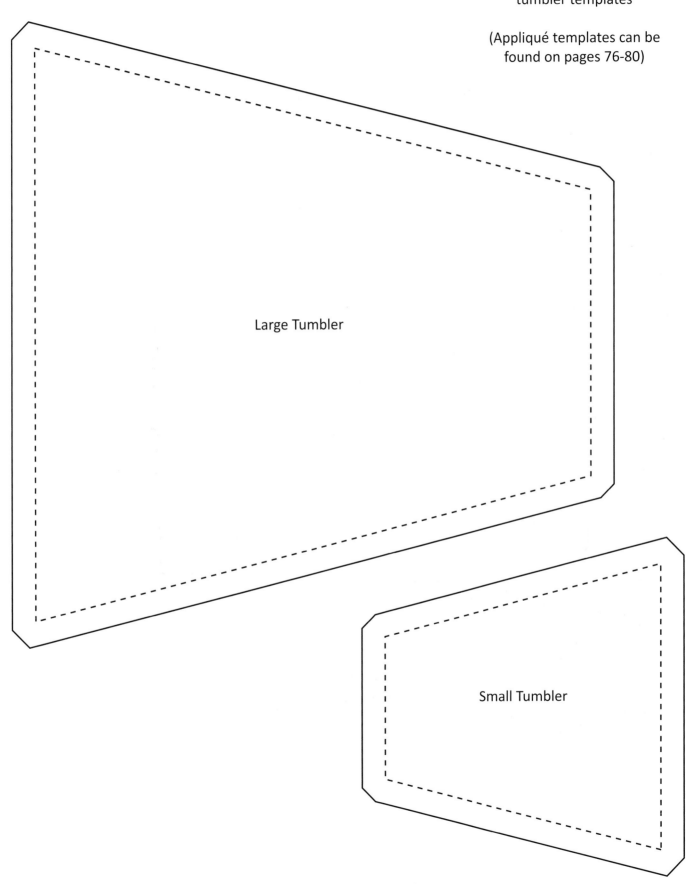

Tumbling We Go
tumbler templates

(Appliqué templates can be
found on pages 76-80)

Large Tumbler

Small Tumbler

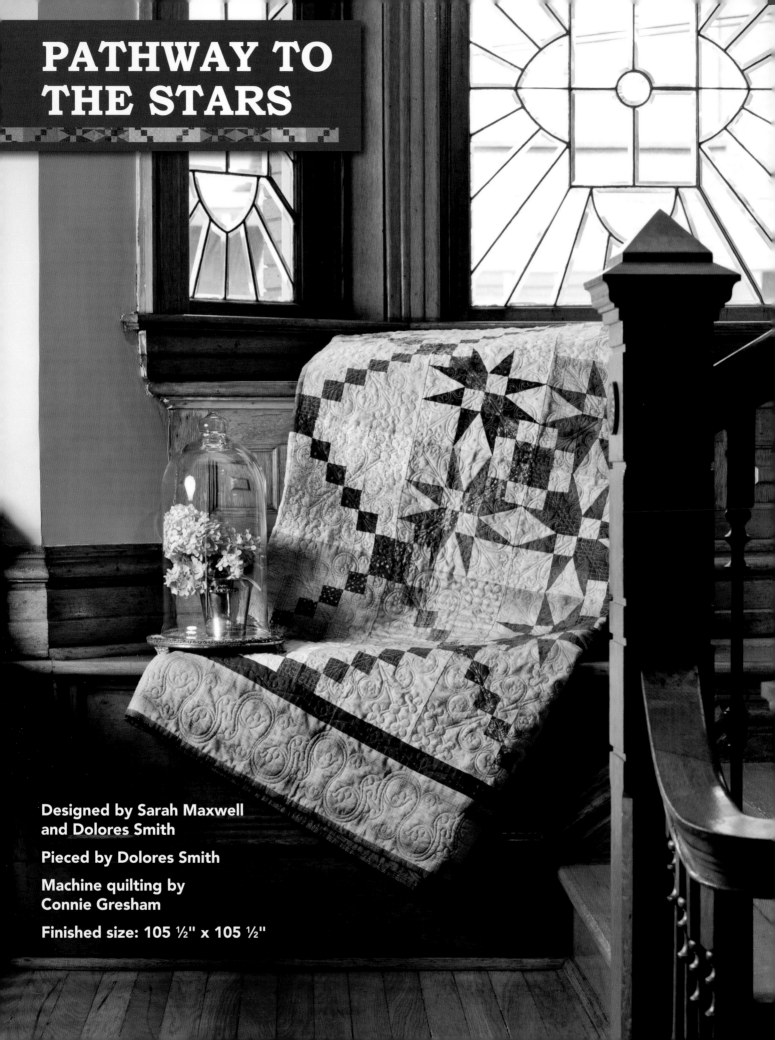

PATHWAY TO THE STARS

**Designed by Sarah Maxwell
and Dolores Smith**

Pieced by Dolores Smith

**Machine quilting by
Connie Gresham**

Finished size: 105 ½" x 105 ½"

Many years ago, Sarah designed this quilt using 1800s fabrics. When I saw the design, I thought it would look great in one of my favorite fabric styles, Japanese taupes. These Japanese fabrics are typically muted, grayed shades of brown, green and blue with an occasional dark red thrown in for an accent. Fabrics can be traditional cotton prints or intricate cotton woven plaids and textures. Combining the prints and plaids adds interest to any project. In general, the taupe prints and woven plaids will work together without a second thought, no matter what color, because they all share that same muted, grayed value.

The original quilt design was made to honor my son Ryan and his soul mate Breigha who left us way too soon. The project sat unfinished for a time. As I worked to finish it for this book, it was a nice time to remember them as well as both my dad and Sarah's dad that we have since lost. It brought back good memories of each one of them and a smile to my face. This is a great design to make as a memory quilt as we can all reflect on pathways to the stars and those who have passed on.

"Pathway to the Stars" is constructed with 44 Garden Patch variation blocks and 56 Carrie Nation blocks, each measuring 9" finished, 9 ½" unfinished.

FABRIC REQUIREMENTS

- 8 yards of assorted light to medium backgrounds for all blocks
- 3 yards of assorted prints for Garden Patch blocks
- 2 yards of assorted red prints for all blocks
- ⅝ yard small brown woven for inner border
- 3 ⅛ yards of taupe woven plaid for outer border (These will be cut LENGTH of fabric)
- 1 yard fabric of choice for binding

CUTTING INSTRUCTIONS

Due to the very scrappy nature of this quilt, cutting instructions are for cutting one block at a time.

Carrie Nation blocks: Select one background and one red fabric for each block.

From **assorted light to medium backgrounds**, cut:
- 6—3 ½" squares
- 6—2" squares

From **assorted red prints**, cut:
- 6—2" squares

Garden Patch Block: Select one background, one print, and one red fabric for each block.

From **assorted light to medium backgrounds**, cut:
- 4 of template B
- 2—3 ½" squares
- 6—2" squares

From **assorted prints**, cut:
- 4 each of template D and E (or Tri-Recs™ tool)

From **assorted red prints**, cut:
- 6—2" squares

Borders and Binding

From **small brown woven**, cut:
- 10—2" strips the width of fabric for inner border

From **taupe woven plaid**, cut:
- 4—6 ½" strips the length of fabric for outer border

From **fabric of choice** for binding, cut:
- 11—2 ½" strips the width of fabric

SEWING INSTRUCTIONS

Refer to the following diagrams to construct one block. We highly recommend using the Tri-Recs™ ruler to construct the star points on the Garden Patch Block. The ruler has detailed instructions on constructing accurate "pointy" points and was indispensable in making this quilt. (Directions on how to use the tool can be found on page 9.) Alternatively, you can choose to use the templates provided in the book.

Garden Patch Block

1 | To make a Garden Patch block, use the Tri-Recs™ Tool to construct the 3 ½" squares with the pointed triangle shape or use the templates provided. This part of the block uses a background fabric and a star point fabric. If you choose to use the templates, use a print fabric for the template D and E. Use the background fabric for template B. See diagram below. Make 4 for each Garden Patch block.

2 | From the matching background and matching assorted red prints sew the 2" squares to make 3 matching sets of four-patch units. Press toward the red prints. See diagram.

3 | Layout the matching background 3 ½" squares, four patch units & star point units and assemble the block as shown. Making sure the four-patch units form a diagonal line through the block. Repeat to make a total of 44 Garden Patch blocks. Press the

seams in each row in alternate directions. The block should measure 9 ½" unfinished.

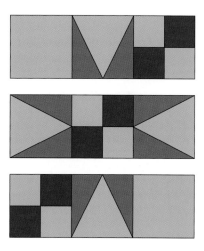

Carrie Nation Block

1 | Sew six matching 2" background squares and six matching 2" red print squares together to form three four-patch units. See diagram below. Press toward the red print.

2 | Assemble the four-patch units and matching background 3 ½" squares as shown in the diagram below so the four-patch units form a diagonal line through the block and piece together to make a Carrie Nation block. Press seams to the left for the top row and alternating to the right for the middle row and then back to the left for bottom row. Repeat for a total of 56 blocks. The block should measure 9 ½" unfinished.

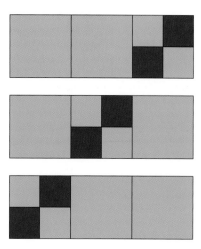

PATHWAY TO THE STARS

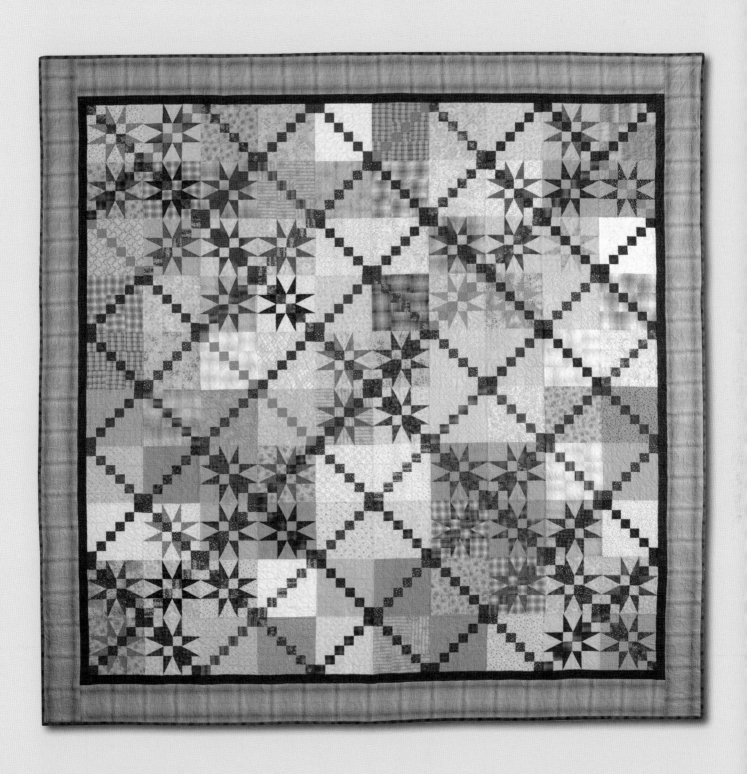

QUILT ASSEMBLY

1 | Referring to the photo of the quilt on page 53 for placement, sew 10 rows of 10 blocks. The first two rows and the last two rows will begin with Garden Patch blocks. Take care with placement of Garden Patch blocks and Carrie Nation blocks in all rows as well as the rotation of the dark red squares in each.

2 | Join the rows to create the quilt center. The top should measure 90 ½" x 90 ½".

3 | Measure the quilt center from the top to bottom through the center. Piece three 2" wide inner border strips end to end, then cut to match that measurement. Repeat to make a second inner border strip. Referring to the quilt assembly diagram, sew these two strips to the sides of the quilt center. Press the seams toward the inner border.

4 | Measure the quilt top from side to side through the center (including the borders you just added). Piece 2" wide inner border print strips end to end, then cut to match that measurement. Repeat to make a second inner border strip. Referring to the

quilt assembly diagram, sew these strips to the top and bottom of the quilt top. Press the seams toward the inner border.

5 | Measure the quilt top from top to bottom through the center. Cut two 6 ½" outer border strips to match this measurement. Sew these two strips to the sides of the quilt center.

6 | Measure the quilt top from side to side through the center (including the borders you just added). Cut the remaining two 6 ½" outer border strips to match this measurement. Sew these to the top and bottom of the quilt. Press seams toward the outer border.

7 | Quilt as desired, then bind.

Pathway to the Stars
templates

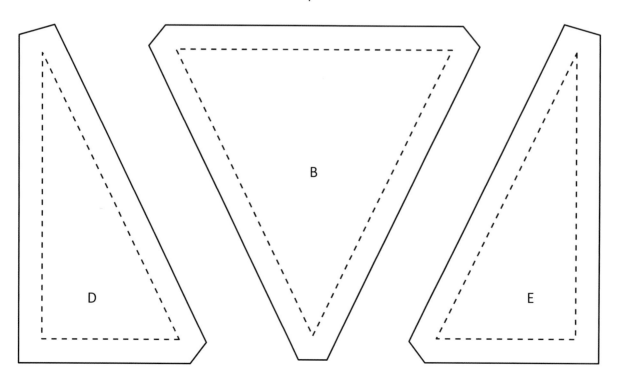

Pathway to the Stars

quilt assembly diagram

SHOOFLY PIE

Designed by Sarah Maxwell

Pieced by Dolores Smith

**Machine quilting by
Connie Gresham**

Finished size: 82 ½" x 91"

Classic, simple blocks remain a favorite way to showcase great fabrics. Sometimes, simpler really is better. Both Dolores and I love the shoofly and churn dash block variations and we've both made numerous quilts using those blocks. For this design, I wanted to highlight how Japanese taupes can include more than just "taupe" colors. In recent years, taupes have expanded to include shades of blue, green, red, peach, pink and purple all subdued by that taupe-y gray tint. Using a traditional dark brown taupe as the anchor fabric in a simple nine-patch block, the design then showcases a range of taupe fabrics in the shoofly block. Each segment of the quilt brings a new color into focus making this a "Shoofly Pie."

The quilt is constructed with 72 shoofly blocks, 56 nine-patch blocks and pieced setting and corner blocks.

FABRIC REQUIREMENTS

- 2 ½ yards total of assorted light/medium prints for shoofly blocks
- 1 ⅝ yards total of assorted medium/dark prints for shoofly blocks
- 2 ¾ yards of light/medium tan woven for nine patches and setting blocks
- 1 ⅞ yards of small-scale dark brown print for nine patches and setting blocks
- ⅞ yard tan woven for inner border
- 2 ½ yards of olive green woven for outer border
- ⅞ yard olive green print for binding

CUTTING INSTRUCTIONS

Due to the scrappy nature of this quilt, cutting instructions are for cutting one block at a time.

Shoofly Block
For each shoofly block, select one light/medium print and one medium/dark print.

From **light/medium print**, cut:
- 2—2 ⅞" squares, cut once on the diagonal for a total of 4 Piece A triangles
- 4—2 ½" squares for a total of 4 Piece B squares

From **medium/dark print**, cut:
- 2—2 ⅞" squares, cut once on the diagonal for a total of 4 Piece A triangles
- 1—2 ½" square (B)

Nine Patch Block
From **light/medium tan woven**, cut:
- 5—2 ½" squares (A)

From **small-scale dark brown print**, cut:
- 4—2 ½" squares (A)

Setting Triangles Block
From **small dark brown print**, cut:
- 2—2 ½" squares (B)

From **light/medium tan woven**, cut:
- 2—2 ⅞" squares, cut once on the diagonal (A) (put the extra triangle (A) aside for later use)
- 1—2 ½" square (B)

Corner Triangle Block
From **small dark brown print**, cut:
- 1—2 ½" square (B)

From **light/medium tan woven**, cut:
- 1—3 ¼" square, cut twice on the diagonal (C) (this will be enough to make all four corner blocks)
- 1—2 ⅞" square, cut once on the diagonal (A)

Borders and Binding
From **tan woven**, cut:
- 12—2" strips for inner border

From **olive green woven**, cut:
- 4—6 ½" by the **length** of fabric for outer border

From **fabric of choice** for binding, cut:
- 9—2 ½" strips the width of fabric

SEWING INSTRUCTIONS

Shoofly Block

1 | With right sides together, layer a light/medium print half-square triangle (A) with a medium/dark print half-square triangle (A). Using a ¼" seam allowance, sew along the long side of the triangles to make a half-square triangle unit. Press toward the medium/dark print. Repeat to make a total of four half-square triangle units. See diagram below.

2 | Referring to the following diagram, sew together four half-square triangle units form step 1, 4—2 ½" light/medium print squares, and a 2 ½" medium/dark print square to create a Shoofly block. Press the seams in top row to the right, middle row to the left, and the bottom row to the right.

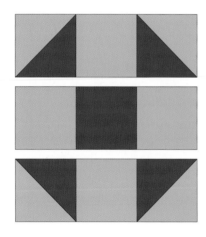

3 | Repeat steps 1—2 to create a total of 72 Shoofly blocks, varying the fabric combinations with each block. Blocks should measure 6 ½" x 6 ½" unfinished, 6" finished.

Nine-Patch Block

1 | Referring to the following diagram, sew together 5—2 ½" light/medium woven square (A) with 4—2 ½" small dark brown print (A) to create a Nine-Patch unit. Press seams toward the small dark brown print.

2 | Repeat to make a total of 56 Nine-Patch blocks. Blocks should measure 6 ½" x 6 ½" unfinished, 6" finished.

Setting Triangle Blocks

1 | Referring to diagram, sew a triangle (A) to the side of one 2 ½" square (B). Press seams toward the left.

2 | Sew another triangle (A) to the opposite of the square (B). Press the seam toward square.

SHOOFLY PIE

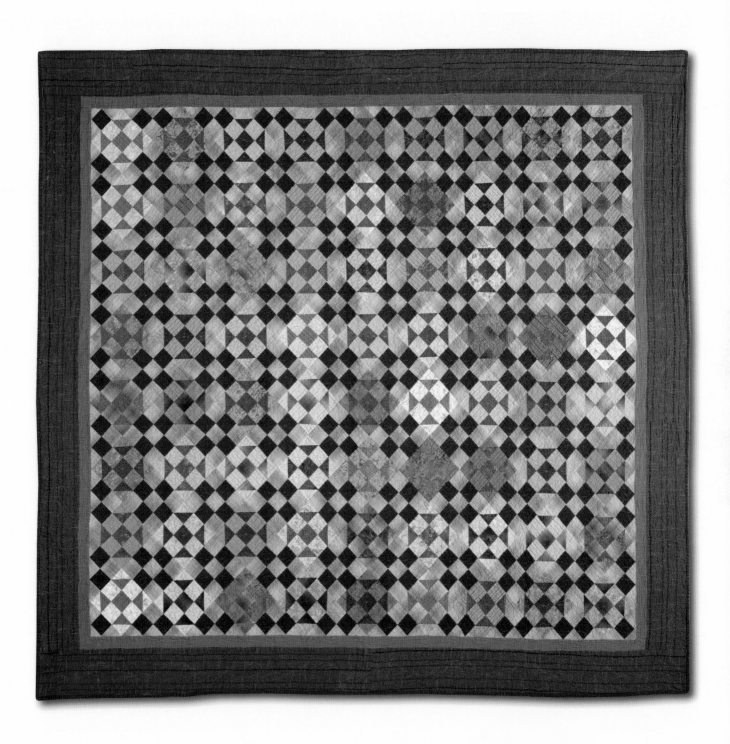

3 | Referring to diagram, sew one 2 ½" medium/dark print square (B) to one 2 ½" light print square (B), then sew one light triangle (A) to the end of the medium/dark print square (B). Press seams toward the right.

4 | Referring to the diagram, sew steps 1—2 together. Press seam toward the bottom of the unit.

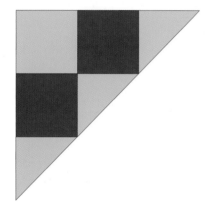

5 | Repeat steps 1—3 to make a total of 30 setting triangle units.

Corner Block

1 | Referring to diagram below, sew two triangle (A) to both sides of a 2 ½" small dark brown print (B). Press toward the triangles.

2 | Referring to diagram below, sew a light triangle (C) to the top of step 1. Repeat steps 1 and 2 for a total of 4 units.

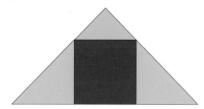

QUILT ASSEMBLY

1 | Referring to the quilt assembly diagram on page 61, layout the blocks, setting triangles and corner triangles.

2 | Referring to the quilt assembly diagram, sew the units from step 1 into diagonal rows, paying careful attention to the orientation of the blocks. Press the seams of each row in alternate directions.

3 | Join the rows to complete the quilt center, which should measure 68" x 76 ¼".

4 | Measure the quilt center from top to bottom through the center. Piece 2" wide tan woven strips end to end, then cut to match that measurement. Repeat to make a second inner border strip. Referring to the quilt assembly diagram, sew these strips to the sides of the quilt center. Press the seams toward the inner border.

5 | Measure the quilt top from side to side through the center (including the borders you just added). Piece 2" wide tan woven strips end to end, then cut to match that measurement. Repeat to make a second inner border strip. Referring to the quilt assembly diagram, sew these two strips to the top and bottom of the quilt top. Press the seams toward the inner border.

6 | Measure the quilt top from top to bottom through the center. Cut a 6 ½" wide olive green strip to match that measurement. Repeat to make a second outer border strip. Referring to the quilt assembly diagram, sew these strips to the sides of the quilt center. Press the seams toward the outer border.

7 | Measure the quilt top from side to side through the center (including the borders you just added). Cut a 6 ½" wide olive green strip to match that measurement. Repeat to make a second outer border strip. Referring to the quilt assembly diagram, sew these strips to the top and bottom of the quilt center. Press the seams toward the outer border.

8 | Quilt as desired, then bind.

Shoofly Pie

quilt assembly diagram

LOG CABIN
TABLE RUNNER

**Designed by Dolores Smith
and Sarah Maxwell**

Pieced by Dolores Smith

Finished size: 14" x 62"

Dolores loves working with wool and finds piecing with it as enjoyable as working with cotton fabrics. A table runner is a great way to try out piecing with wool to see if you love it too!

WOOL REQUIREMENTS

Use felted wool.

- 12" x 14" light teal for Block A
- 14" x 18" dark teal for Block A
- 14" x 26" purple for Block A
- 10" x 12" green for Block B
- 10" x 18" light gold for Block B
- 14" x 18" dark gold for Block B
- 9" x 65" black wool for border and all block centers
- 1 ½ yards black flannel for backing and binding

CUTTING INSTRUCTIONS

For all blocks.

Block A: Make 3
From **black**, cut:
- 3—Piece A, 3 ½" square (center)

From **light teal**, cut:
- 3—Piece B, 2" x 3 ½"
- 6—Piece C, 2" x 5"
- 3—Piece D, 2" x 6 ½"

From **dark teal**, cut:
- 3—Piece E, 2" x 6 ½"
- 6—Piece F, 2" x 8"
- 3—Piece G, 2" x 9 ½"

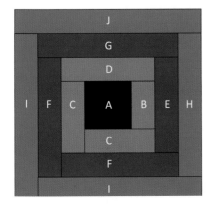

63

From **purple**, cut:
- 3—Piece H, 2" x 9 ½"
- 6—Piece I, 2" x 11"
- 3—Piece J, 2" x 12 ½"

Block B: Make 2
From **black**, cut:
- 2—Piece A, 3 ½" square (center)

From **green**, cut:
- 2—Piece B, 2" x 3 ½"
- 4—Piece C, 2" x 5"
- 2—Piece D, 2" x 6 ½"

From **light gold**, cut:
- 2—Piece E, 2" x 6 ½"
- 4—Piece F, 2" x 8"
- 2—Piece G, 2" x 9 ½"

From **dark gold**, cut:
- 2—Piece H, 2" x 9 ½"
- 4—Piece I, 2" x 11"
- 2—Piece J, 2" x 12 ½"

Borders
From **black**, cut:
- 2—1 ½" x 12 ½" (ends)
- 2—1 ½" x 62 ½" (top and bottom)

SEWING INSTRUCTIONS

Please note that when sewing with wool it does stretch, so take extra care and don't pull.

Block A
Sewing instructions for one block. (Make 3)

1 | Referring to diagram below, sew a piece B light teal to the right side of piece A black (center). Press seams open.

2 | Referring to the diagram below, sew one piece C light teal to the bottom and press seams open. Sew one piece C light teal to the left side and press seams open.

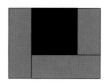

3 | Referring to the diagram below, sew piece D light teal to the top. Press seams open. The unit should measure at this point 6 ½" x 6 ½". Please note that wool does stretch, so square it to the measurement.

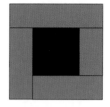

4 | Referring to the diagram below, sew piece E dark teal to the right side. Press seams open.

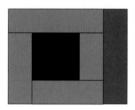

5 | Referring to the diagram below, sew one piece F dark teal to the bottom and press seams open. Sew one piece F dark teal to the left side and press seams open.

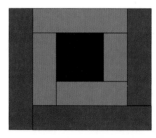

6 | Referring to diagram below, sew piece G dark teal to the top of the unit. Press seams open. Now the unit should measure 9 ½" x 9 ½".

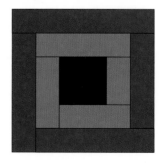

7 | Referring to the diagram below, sew piece H purple to the right side. Press seams open.

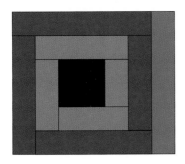

8 | Referring to the diagram below, sew one piece I purple to the bottom and press seams open. Sew one piece I purple to the left side and press seams open.

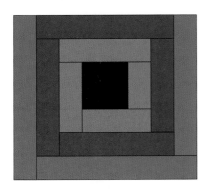

9 | Referring to the diagram below, sew piece J purple to the top of the unit. Press seams open. The block should measure 12 ½" x 12 ½".

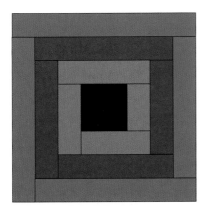

Block B

Sewing instructions for one block. (Make 2)

1 | Referring to diagram below, sew a piece B green to the right side of piece A black (center). Press seams open.

2 | Referring to the diagram below, sew one piece C green to the bottom and press seams open. Sew one piece C green to the left side and press seams open.

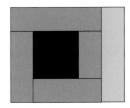

3 | Referring to the diagram below, sew piece D green to the top. Press seams open. The unit should measure at this point 6 ½" x 6 ½". Please note that wool does stretch, so square it to the measurement.

4 | Referring to the diagram below, sew piece E light gold to the right side. Press seams open.

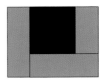

5 | Referring to the diagram below, sew one piece F light gold to the bottom and press seams open. Sew one piece F light gold to the left side and press seams open.

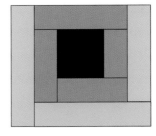

6 | Referring to diagram below, sew piece G light gold to the top of the unit. Press seams open. Now the unit should measure 9 ½" x 9 ½".

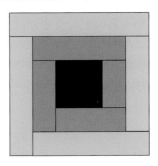

7 | Referring to the diagram below, sew piece H dark gold to the right side. Press seams open.

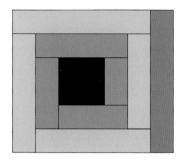

8 | Referring to the diagram below, sew one piece I dark gold to the bottom and press seams open. Sew one piece I dark gold to the left side and press seams open.

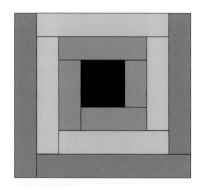

9 | Referring to the diagram below, sew piece J dark gold to the top of the unit. Press seams open. The block should measure 12 ½" x 12 ½".

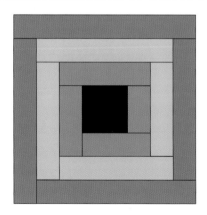

ASSEMBLY INSTRUCTIONS

1 | Starting with a Block A, sew blocks together, alternating Block A and Block B until you have all 5 blocks sewn together. All blocks should have piece J on the top. The runner should measure 12 ½" x 60 ½".

2 | Add two 1 ½" x 12 ½" end pieces of black wool to both ends of the runner. Press seams open. Sew the remaining top and bottom pieces of black wool on. Press seams open.

3 | Quilt and bind as desired. I chose to just quilt in the center black square of each block.

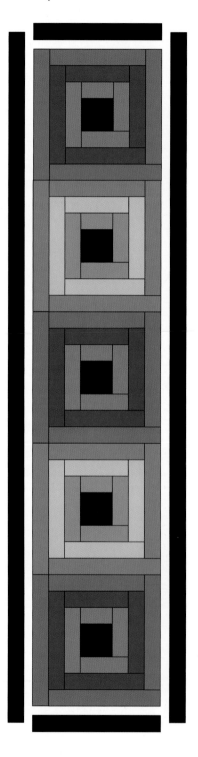

Log Cabin Table Runner

quilt assembly diagram

66

SIMPLIFY

**Designed and made by
Dolores Smith**

Finished size: 63" x 22"

*Combining her love of wool with woven plaids, Dolores created the "Simplify"
runner to serve as a homespun accent on a dining room table. The offset
lettering creates interest while the sunflowers brighten any day.*

SUPPLY LIST

- 2 yards of green plaid fabric for front
- 2 yards of brown/gold flannel for back
- ⅓ yard dark green plaid fabric for flying geese

I used all hand-dyed wool
- 12" x 35" light gold wool for letters
- 6" x 42" gold wool for sunflower petals
- 7" x 14" brown wool for sunflower center

- Steam-A-Seam®
- Matching floss: *I use Valdani*

CUTTING INSTRUCTIONS

From **dark green plaid**, cut:
- 18—4 ½" squares for flying geese
- 1—22 ½" x 63 ½" rectangle for front

From **brown/gold flannel** cut:
- 1—22 ½" x 63 ½" rectangle for back

ASSEMBLY INSTRUCTIONS

1 | Follow the manufacturer's instructions for
Steam-A-Seam. Trace the letters, sunflower petals
and flower centers on the side with adhesive. Cut
around the pieces leaving about ⅛" past the traced
lines of the designs. Peel the non-adhesive paper
away. Following the manufacturer's instructions,
press the patterns on to the wool, picking up the
iron and testing to be sure the adhesive has adhered
to the wool. Once the fabric has cooled, cut out the
design on the traced line.

2 | Refer to the table runner pictures on pages 69
and 70 for placement of the wool pieces. Peel the
paper off the back of the wool pieces and place
them on the green plaid. Once you are satisfied with
their placement, press in place with the adhesive
side down. Continue pressing until they are
adhered in place. With matching thread, use a whip
stitch to sew the pieces in place.

3 | Take the 18—4 ½" squares from the dark
green plaid and fold the squares in half, wrong sides
together. Then take both sides and fold toward the
middle and press.

4 | Baste nine of the flying geese to the ends of the table runner, overlapping each flying geese unit until they are across both ends. See picture to the right. Make sure to place the flying geese with the tops pointing towards the center of the table runner.

5 | Now, you are ready to put the runner together. Layer the backing on top of the appliquéd runner, right sides together. Sew around the runner leaving an opening. Turn right side out through the opening and press, taking care to ensure the raw edge of the opening is pressed in. Top stitch around the entire runner with an ⅛" seam.

Each of the sunflowers are a little different, just like in nature. Arrange the petals and layer them as you wish.

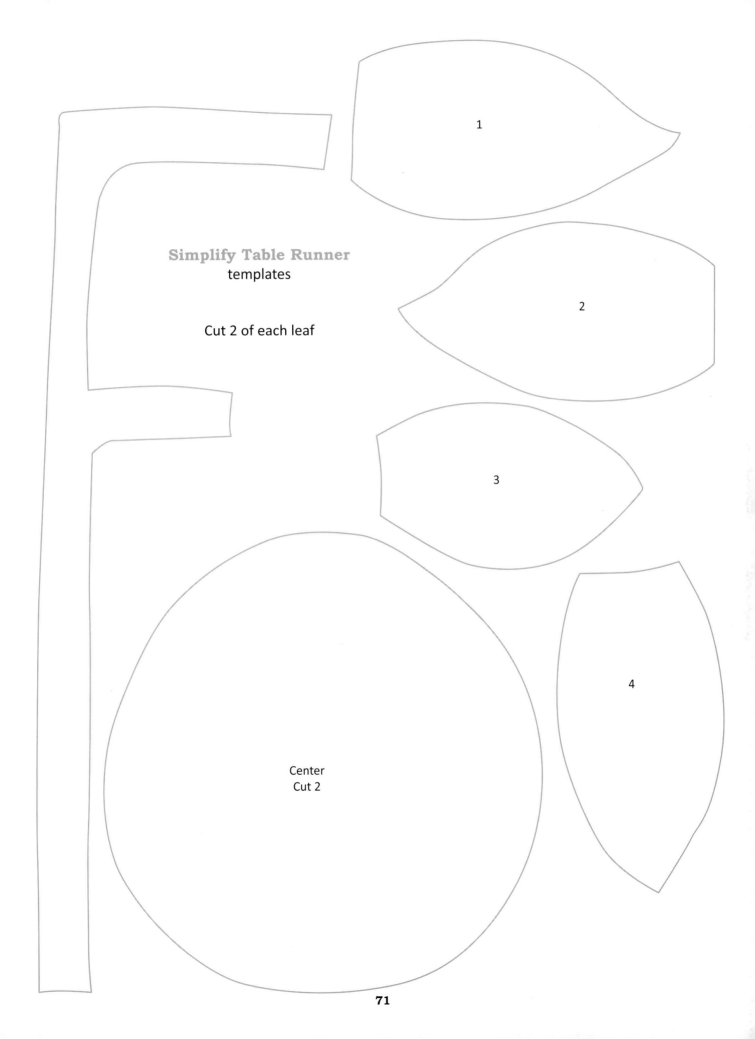

Simplify Table Runner
templates

Cut 2 of each leaf

1

2

3

4

Center
Cut 2

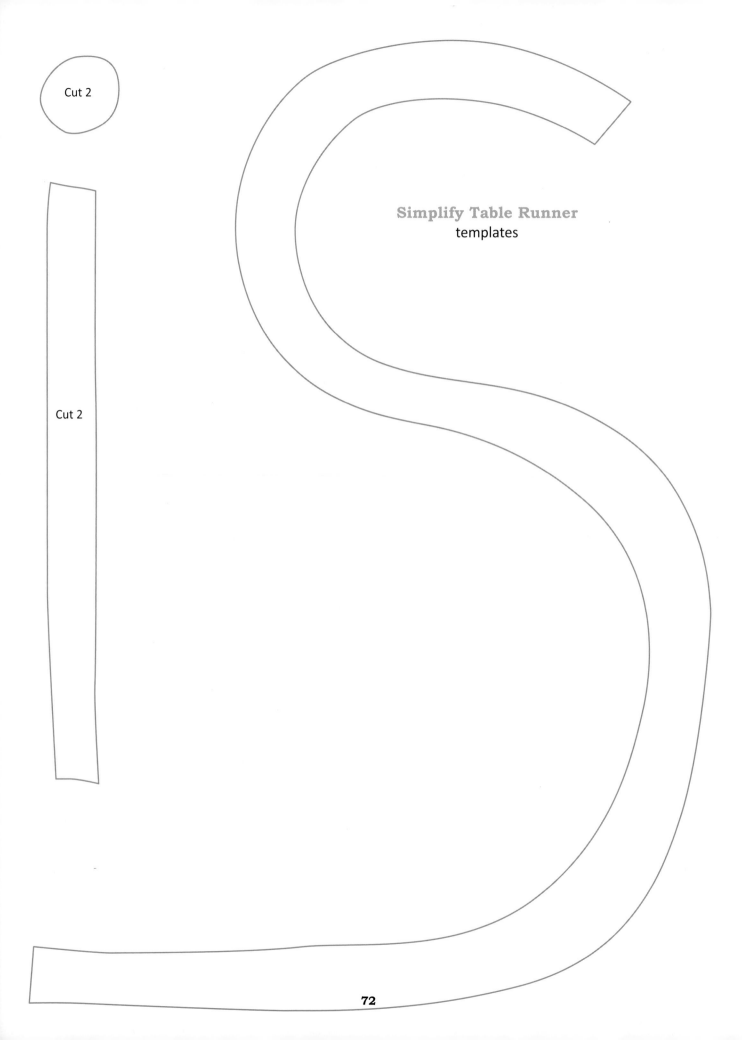

Cut 2

Cut 2

Simplify Table Runner
templates

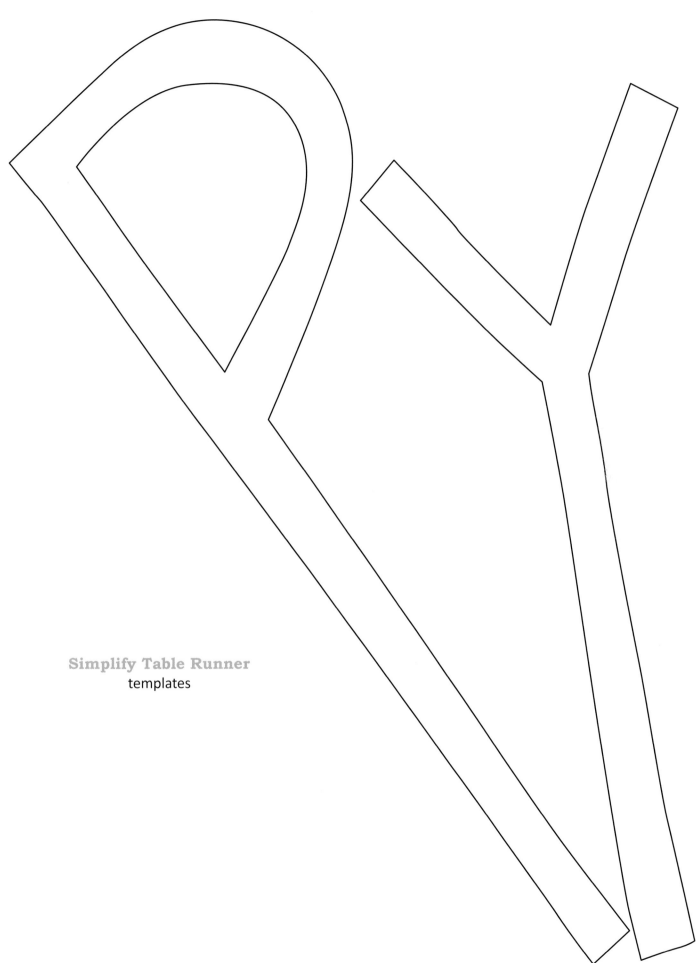

Simplify Table Runner
templates

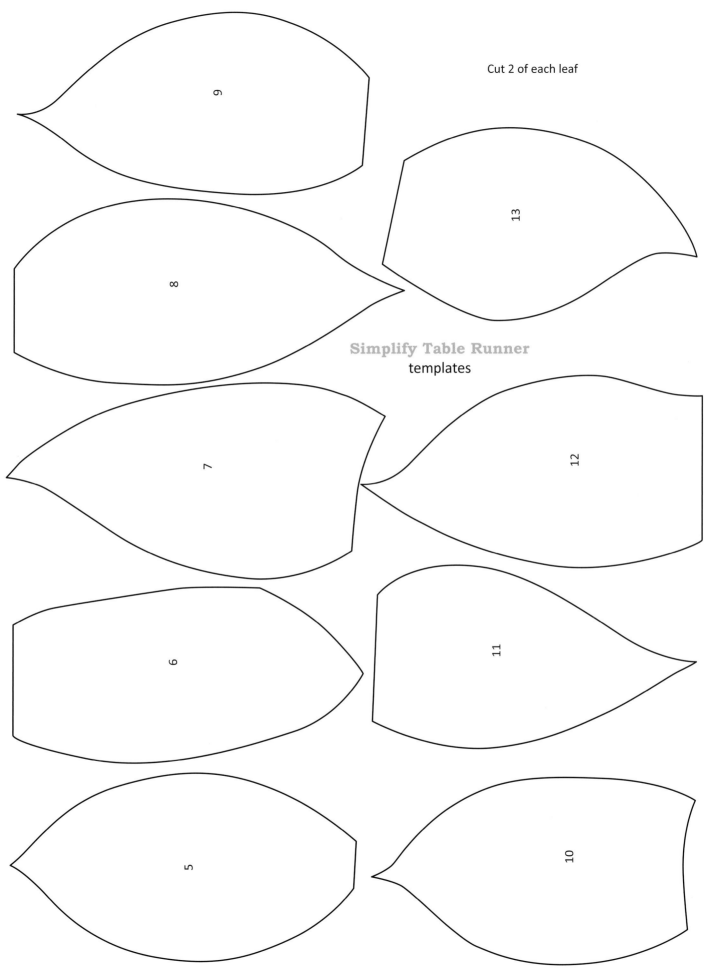

Cut 2 of each leaf

Simplify Table Runner
templates

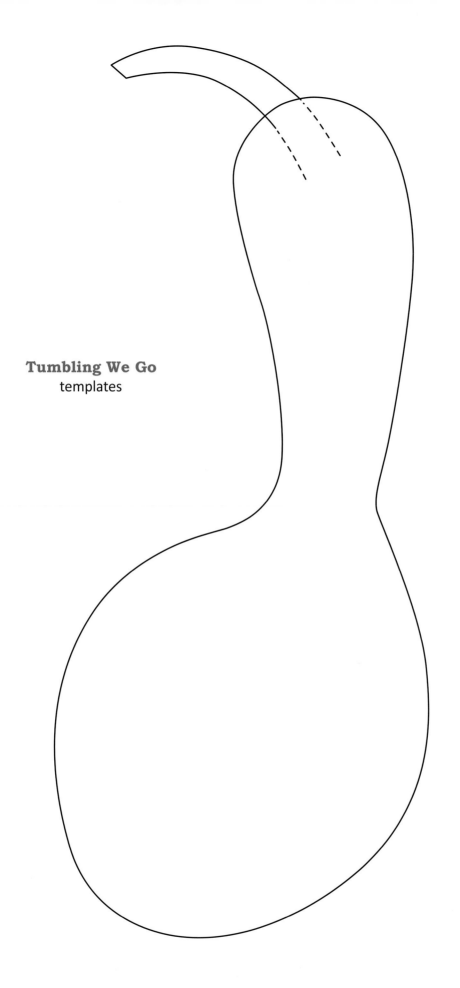

Tumbling We Go
templates

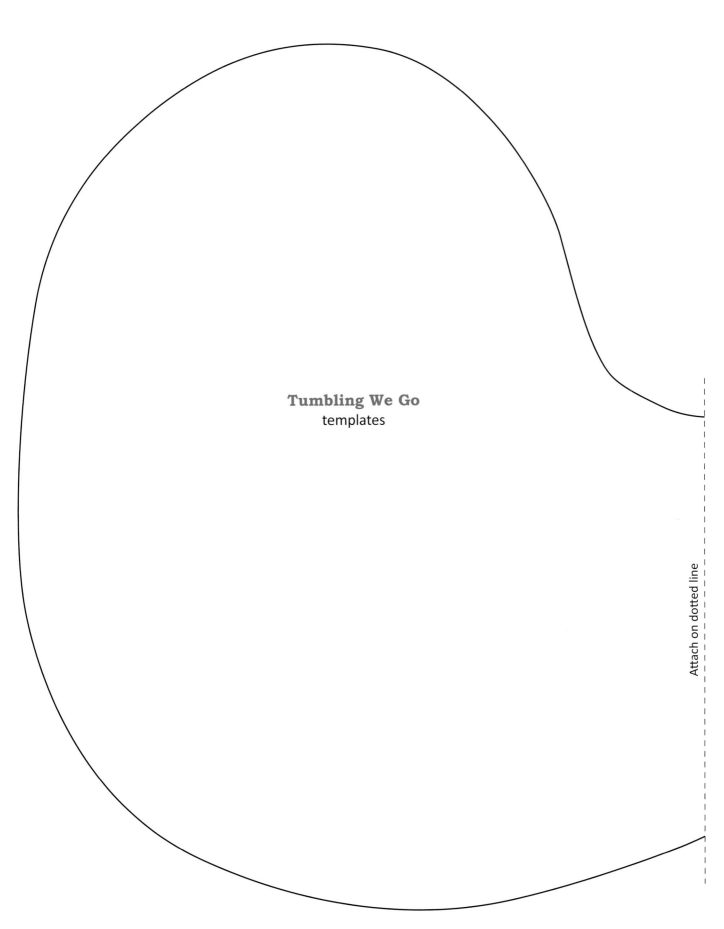

Tumbling We Go
templates

Attach on dotted line

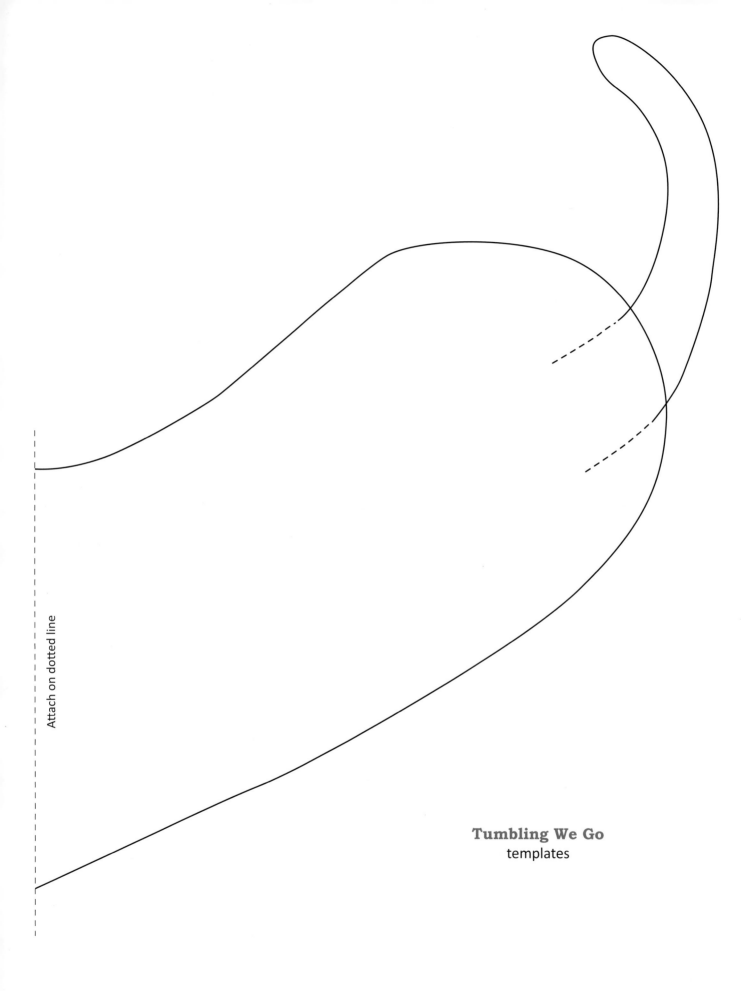

Attach on dotted line

Tumbling We Go
templates

Tumbling We Go
templates

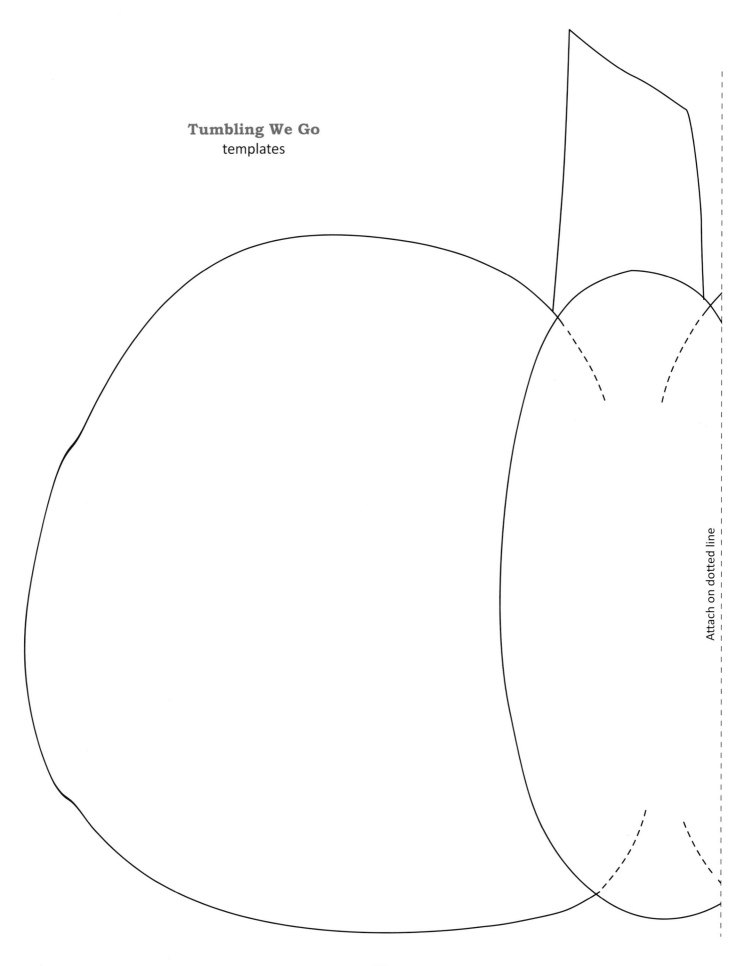

Attach on dotted line

Tumbling We Go
templates

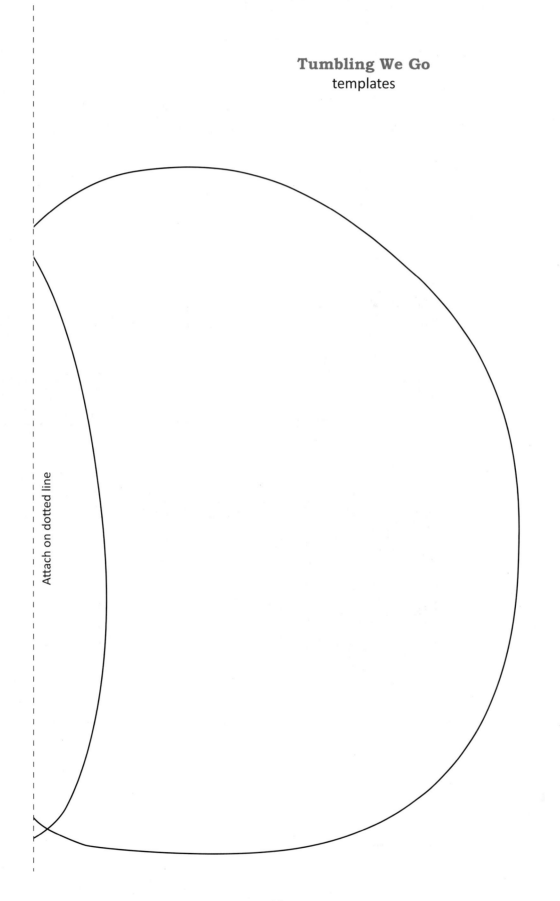

Attach on dotted line